Karl Polanyi on Ethics and Economics

Breaking new ground in Polanyi scholarship, Gregory Baum explores the relation between ethics, culture, and economics in Karl Polanyi's writings. He identifies and analyses key concepts of Polanyi's thought and shows how they apply to the contemporary debate on ethics and economics.

Exploring Polanyi's lesser-known works as well as *The Great Transformation*, Baum provides a more complete and nuanced understanding of Polanyi's thought. He examines Polanyi's interpretation of modern economic and social history, clarifies the ethical presuppositions present in Polanyi's work, and shows how Polanyi's understanding of the relation between ethics and economics touches on many issues relevant to the contemporary debate about the world's economic future. He argues that we should look to Polanyi's understanding of modern capitalism to reinstate the social discourse and, in political practice, the principles of reciprocity and solidarity and points to examples, both in Canada and abroad, of attempts to formulate alternative models of economic development and to create new forms of institutional and cultural intervention.

Karl Polanyi on Ethics and Economics provides fascinating insights into Polanyi's work and today's central social and political issues. It will be of great interest to sociologists, economists, political scientists, and philosophers.

GREGORY BAUM is professor emeritus of theological ethics and sociology of religion, McGill University.

Karl Polanyi on Ethics and Economics

Gregory Baum

McGill-Queen's University Press
Montreal & Kingston • London • Buffalo

ISBN 0-7735-1395-7 (cloth)
ISBN 0-7735-1396-5 (paper)

Legal deposit first quarter 1996
Bibliothèque nationale du Québec

Printed in Canada on acid-free paper

McGill-Queen's University Press is grateful
to the Canada Council
for support of its publishing program.

Cataloguing in Publication Data

Baum, Gregory, 1923–
Karl Polanyi on ethics and economics.
Includes bibliographical references.
ISBN 0-7735-1395-7 (bound) –
ISBN 0-7735-1396-5 (pbk.)
1. Polanyi, Karl, 1886–1964. 2. Economics – Moral and
ethical aspects. I. Title.
HB72.B34 1996 330'.092 C95-920889-5

Typeset in Adobe Garamond 10.5/13
by Caractéra inc., Quebec City

Contents

Foreword

There is currently widespread interest in the work of Karl Polanyi among progressive thinkers, activists, and a growing community of heterodox social scientists. Although *The Great Transformation*, published in 1944, is acclaimed in France as one of the ten classics of twentieth-century social thought and has been translated into eight languages, Polanyi's influence within North America was, until recently, largely within the discipline of anthropology. Those who acknowledged the broader significance of his writings to contemporary social thought were marginalized by the intellectual community.

The publication of *Trade and Markets in the Early Empires* in 1958 launched a historic debate in anthropology and led to the establishment of two rival schools of thought within this discipline. Polanyi's followers, the substantivists, emphasized the role of culture, history, and institutions in the economic life of so-called primitive and archaic societies. The opposing formalist school defended the prevailing neo-classical economic orthodoxy. Although this debate raged in the pages of major anthropological journals in the 1960s, Polanyi received little recognition elsewhere. His analysis of non-market societies shook the discipline of anthropology, which was firmly committed to the universality of the principles underlying neo-classical economic theory, but the more radical conclusion of *The Great Transformation*, that these principles were universally inappropriate – for market as well as non-market economies – was not part of the debate. Polanyi's work rarely appeared on an economic syllabus; instead, the counterpoise to neoclassical orthodoxy was a vulgar Marxism. On the Marxist left Polanyi was considered to be a "circulationist" whose focus was on exchange and not on relations of production. The emphasis he placed on social and cultural dislocation further alienated him from the Marxist left.

How do we explain the current Polanyi revival? Polanyi's thesis that there can be no self-regulating market was confirmed by nineteenth-century liberalism, which enshrined a set of ideals it could not put into practice. The principles of *laissez-faire* prevailed despite the contradictory need for an institutional framework to protect society from the ravages of a free market economy and to establish the very conditions without which the economy could not function. *Laissez-faire* was quickly reduced to an ideology without a corresponding practice. It is that historic duplicity which guides policy makers today.

The international financial crisis and the depression of the 1920s and 1930s led to the welfare state and Keynesian economic policy, both to preserve capitalism and to protect those who were unable to participate fully in economic life. Sadly, the return of nineteenth-century ideals as we approach the end of the twentieth century is less hopeful. The "place of the economy in society" is not considered in a world driven by principles that have been stripped bare of their history. It is in this environment that progressive thinkers are discovering or rediscovering Karl Polanyi.

In 1986 the First International Karl Polanyi Conference was held in Budapest to commemorate the centenary of Polanyi's birth. Papers were presented by historians, economists, political scientists, anthropologists, sociologists, and Hungarian political figures and intellectuals, among others. The presence of political figures and intellectuals reveals a great deal about the previously ambiguous reception of Polanyi. Because he was a socialist, communist intellectuals in Hungary paid tribute to Polanyi's work while ignoring his earlier critical writings on central planning and economic determinism. At the same time, however, dissident intellectuals in Hungary were discovering Polanyi as an important ally in their struggle against communism.

The collapse of communism in Eastern Europe in 1989 should have heightened interest in Polanyi's work in this part of the world. This did not happen. Instead the neo-liberal agenda adopted in the West for more than a decade, complete with its documented failures and contradictions, went unchallenged and indeed was embraced as the road to freedom. Polanyi's influence, celebrated only three years earlier in Hungary, was forgotten. The social degradation of nineteenth-century industrial capitalism so poignantly described in *The Great Transformation* was ignored as these countries, one by one, adopted the principles of *laissez-faire.*

Instead of the promised prosperity, Eastern Europe and the former Soviet Union are now experiencing widespread poverty, violence, and growing social malaise. The recent democratic election of communist parties in several countries comes as no surprise. They can only look back to their pasts, not toward the West, which has no lessons to impart. It took these events to spark a revival of the dialogue about Polanyi begun in 1986 in Budapest.

Those of us who returned to the West following the 1986 centenary began to establish the means to broaden Polanyi's influence among intellectuals and activists. The response was overwhelming. This counter-movement to the hegemonic discourse of the right led to the establishment in 1988 of the Karl Polanyi Institute of Political Economy at Concordia University in Montreal. In a short period of time the Institute created an international network of scholars and activists that offers a vital intellectual space for critical social thought.

In the late 1980s I met Gregory Baum, who had recently arrived in Quebec. He welcomed the establishment of an independent institute for progressive scholarship and became actively engaged in all aspects of its life. His enthusiasm has been a driving force behind the many events the Institute continues to hold – from its Club Jeudi suppers, at which he has led many discussions, to our international conferences and publications. His commitment to the Institute has been important to its continued existence. With the Institute's founders and friends, he has helped to develop a unique interdisciplinary intellectual environment in Quebec.

Two summers ago Gregory Baum was a resident scholar at the Karl Polanyi Institute. Inspired by many discussions with Kari Polanyi Levitt about her father's early writings in German on fascism and socialism, he decided to research these documents. As our offices were next door to each other, I was privileged to discover these works with Professor Baum as he generously shared his readings and reflections with me. He was fascinated by the material and eager to communicate it to a wider audience. His findings were first presented in a lecture series – the Sproul Lectures – at McGill University in 1993 and are now woven into this book.

For Gregory Baum, Polanyi's early writings contribute significantly to his own "ongoing involvement in the church and [an] uninterrupted dialogue with critical social science." In the pages that follow he presents new insights into Polanyi's thought and advances a powerful argument against the philosophy of individualism that governs people's lives today. We need a new ethics of responsibility, Professor Baum writes, which can be found in Polanyi's ethics applied to present circumstances, particularly Polanyi's concept of the *Lebensweg*, the day-to-day ethical task of living that is so severely compromised in a society dominated by material gain. Polanyi believed that the repository of social creativity lies in the culture of the common people, a creativity that today is expressed in the resistance to neo-liberal orthodoxy by progressive social movements. Although much has been written about these emerging democratic alternatives, a new theoretical perspective within which they can be understood is lacking. In *Karl Polanyi on Ethics and Economics*, Professor Baum breaks this intellectual impasse.

A critical discourse that speaks to the dehumanizing cultural consequences of the free market system is vitally needed today. Gregory Baum has found this discourse in Karl Polanyi's writings, adding to it a theory of ethics that is rooted in Enlightenment values and Christian social thought to show that only if people are free to live an ethical life can there be social or societal freedom – *gesellschaftliche Freiheit.* Professor Baum's compelling analysis is a critical contribution to an intellectual counter-movement in which he himself is a leading figure.

Marguerite Mendell
Concordia University, Montreal

Preface

So much has happened in the world over the last decade that we seem to be living in a new age. The Gulf War of 1991 shattered hopes for a more peaceful world. At the same time, the collapse of the Soviet bloc communist regimes substantially transformed the geography of power in the world, while the collapse of Marxism and the decline of the Left have occasioned the waning of human solidarity in social theory and political practice. Contemporary capitalism, meanwhile, is revealing its inner contradictions by producing massive unemployment and economic disarray in the developed nations and allowing misery to worsen in the less developed world. The spread of that misery generates waves of emigrants and refugees and makes those who remain at home increasingly angry and restless. Even in the relatively prosperous West, people pushed to the margin are becoming angrier and the government's reaction to them meaner. Finally, the ecological crisis is impinging on our conscience as never before and raising questions we are not yet prepared to answer.

Today social scientists wonder whether their inherited concepts are adequate for the interpretation of what is taking place in the world. On what wisdom should they draw in their response to contemporary conditions? "Have we read the wrong authors?" asks a Canadian political scientist.[1] Were there important thinkers whom we did not take seriously enough because at the time they did not fit into the dominant framework? Can we derive help from scholars whom we read too quickly in the past?

Standing out in the current revival of long-neglected authors is Karl Polanyi, economist, economic historian, and anthropologist, whose magnum opus, *The Great Transformation*, published in 1944 and translated into many languages, is gradually becoming a classic in social science and political economy. Born in Vienna, Polanyi lived and worked in Hungary, Austria, England, and, from 1950 on, in Canada, where he died in 1964. His brilliant analysis of the crisis of our times, explored in many publications, is now receiving wide attention among scholars belonging to several disciplines.[2] Original in his political economy is the importance he attaches to ethical values and cultural issues.

In Montreal, Kari Levitt, professor emeritus of McGill University, and Marguerite Mendell, professor of economics at Concordia University, have founded the Karl Polanyi Institute of Political Economy, which promotes dialogue and interdisciplinary research regarding the present social and economic crisis by taking seriously – as did Polanyi – the role of culture and the need for ethics. I became a member of this institute soon after I arrived in Montreal in 1986 to take up a teaching position in the Faculty of Religious Studies at McGill University.

In 1993 I was invited by my faculty to give the Sproule lectures on Christian ethics, offered in February of each year. Since social ethics – the subject I teach at McGill – is a discipline engaged in dialogue with social, economic, and political theory, I decided to address in my lectures the contemporary relevance of Karl Polanyi's work. The present book represents a slighty edited version of these lectures.

In chapter 1 I present Polanyi's original and now celebrated theory of "the double movement," introduced and demonstrated in *The Great Transformation.* The scholarly commentary on Polanyi's social theory is ample, but his work has rarely been examined from the perspective of social ethics.[3] This is what I attempt to do. In the second chapter I examine the ethical foundation of Karl Polanyi's thought. Although he did not write as a professional philosopher, he held that humans had an ethical vocation and that ethics played an essential role in the making of society and in the scientific endeavour to understand it. In chapter 3 I investigate to what extent Polanyi's social theory is relevant to the historical conditions of the present. Since Polanyi thought that humanity was addressed by a universal call to solidarity, responsibility, and respect for nature, I examine in the final chapter whether there are resources for such an ethic in today's liberal, pluralistic society.

I do not wish to close this preface without thanking Dean Donna Runnalls of McGill's Faculty of Religious Studies for the support she has given me over the years in my activities as an author and editor; and Professor Marguerite Mendell of Concordia University, currently the director of the Karl Polanyi Institute, for her challenging ideas and her friendship.

Gregory Baum
Montreal, Quebec

Karl Polanyi on Ethics and Economics

I

Polanyi's Theory of the Double Movement

In *The Great Transformation*, Karl Polanyi analyses the crisis of modern society. He does not claim that his idea is wholly original, for he finds aspects of it in the thought of the nineteenth-century social reformer Robert Owen. Owen argued that the new capitalism had caused not simply the material impoverishment of the workers but also the disruption of the ethical culture to which they belonged and through which they defined their identity. He was among the first to recognize that economic institutions have an impact on people's cultural self-understanding. He advocated – and actually established – an alternative organization of industrial production, one that allowed workers to define their lives through mutual respect and cooperation. These were ideas that Polanyi pursued in a systematic way.

In *The Great Transformation* Polanyi offers a critical examination of the industrial capitalism set up in England in the early part of the nineteenth century. Whereas Karl Marx accused capitalism of exploiting workers, Polanyi – without denying this – concentrates on the dehumanizing cultural consequences of the free market system. The predominance of the unregulated market removed people from the sociocultural framework which constituted the matrix of their human existence. In the past, Polanyi argues, economic activity was embedded in the social relations that made up the community as a whole. What was new and startling with the self-regulating market was that it "disembedded" the economy from its social base, created widespread cultural alienation among workers and owners, and left society and the natural environment without protection. This "disembedding" of economic activity from people's social relations remains a key concept in Polanyi's analysis.

The self-regulating market, advocated in England at the end of the eighteenth century and legally constituted by the Poor Law Reform Act in 1834, was a *novum* in human history. Polanyi analyses the destructive impact of the new economic system by focusing on the transformation of labour and land into market commodities. In the new industrial capitalism, both labour (human beings) and land (the natural endowment) were bought and sold, used and destroyed, as if they were simply merchandise, even though they were in no sense the products of human industry. They were commodities only fictitiously. With regard to the commodification of "land," Polanyi, as early as the 1940s, draws attention to the ecological devastation produced by the self-regulating market. "Nature would be reduced to its elements, neighbourhoods and landscapes defiled, rivers polluted … and the power to produce food and raw materials destroyed."[1]

In his critique of the emerging economy, Polanyi – as we shall see – transcends the traditional debate between capitalism and socialism. In fact, he rarely uses the word "capitalism." The object of his sustained criticism is the self-regulating market system. Polanyi holds that markets are important institutions: complex societies cannot get along without them. He has no sympathy whatsoever for the centralized command economy advocated by and practised in the communist Soviet Union. Yet he distinguishes between markets and the market system, that is to say, the integration of all markets into a single national or international economy. The market system is a modern phenomenon. What concerns Polanyi, and what he criticizes vigorously, is the self-regulating market system – a market economy unconstrained by society and operating simply according to its own law of supply and demand.

Polanyi's examination of industrial capitalism in nineteenth-century England does not stop at this negative result. He shows in great detail that, after a relatively short period during which the market remained unregulated, a political and cultural counter-movement emerged in England. Originating in the late 1840s, this movement sought to protect society – both its people and the land – from unrestrained market forces. "Not until 1834," Polanyi writes, "was a competitive labour market established in England; hence, industrial capitalism as a social system cannot be said to have existed before that date. Yet almost immediately the self-protection of society set in: factory laws and social legislation, and a political and industrial working class movement sprang into being. It was in this attempt to stave off the entirely new dangers of the market mechanism that protective action conflicted fatally with the self-regulation of the system."[2]

Polanyi argues that the self-regulating market is a new human invention for which there are no parallels in past history. But new does not mean progressive. Greater sanity belongs to the earlier phases of human development when economic activity exercised a social function and thus helped to constitute society as a whole. Labour was then embedded in social relations. The production and distribution of goods in tribal, feudal, and mercantile societies did not create a separate economic system. Polanyi claims that the self-regulating market, created by state intervention, was so foreign to human ways and so devastating in its consequences that it provoked almost immediately a significant counter-current that sought to protect society and the land.

The conclusion at which Polanyi arrives, then, is that modern capitalist society is characterized by "a double movement": on the one hand, the self-regulating market supported by the owning and trading classes, and, on the other, the safeguarding of society by social forces that seek to protect the people, their land, and their culture. Sometimes he speaks of the first movement as seeking blind "economic improvement" and of the second as protecting "habitation."[3]

Because of this double movement, Polanyi argues, modern industrial society, despite the newness of the free market, remains in continuity with the great social orders of the past. Modern society continues to protect itself against the forces that undermine its social solidarity and threaten to distort its relationship to the natural environment. This counter-movement is what Polanyi calls the Great Transformation.

Is the double movement a theory that can be trusted? Are there social forces in our day that move against the stream and seek to protect people and safeguard habitation? When I first read Karl Polanyi, I asked myself whether this great economic historian was a functionalist social thinker who, like Emile Durkheim, looked upon society as an organic unit that would, whenever disturbed, return to equilibrium by its own inner vitality.[4] Such assumptions about the nature of society are, in my mind, unwarranted. By contrast, some students of Polanyi have suggested that his theory of the double movement was inspired by a dialectical understanding of history in the tradition of Hegel and Marx. Did Polanyi believe in necessary progress?

For the Christian ethicist these are important questions. Both functionalist and dialectical theory presuppose that history moves according to certain laws, that the direction of human development is predictable, and that the human enterprise is governed by necessity. Christian thinkers – with very few exceptions – take a much different view. For Christians, history remains always open, open to the self-chosen, human destructiveness called "sin" and open to the surprising powers of generosity and reconciliation called "divine grace." The course of human history cannot be predicted by science. What the sciences can discover in historical developments are currents or trends, not laws; and on the strength of these trends, scientists are able to make modest predictions, suggest what is likely to happen, and propose courses of action that promise to serve human well-being.

Is Polanyi's work based on necessity or freedom? To reply to this question, we must analyse in greater detail the demonstration he offers for his theory of the double movement. In *The Great Transformation* Polanyi proposes two distict arguments, one historical and the other anthropological. The first argument he draws from his research into the economic and social history of England from the late eighteenth century to the end of the nineteenth century. Here he shows that the concrete history of one country, the country in which industrialization began, was the locus of the double movement.

The second argument is of a different kind. Here Polanyi appeals to what he calls "the changelessness of man as a social being."[5] Relying on extensive anthropological research, he demonstrates that throughout known human history economic activity has always been embedded in social relations. Since the self-regulating market, a unique and unparalleled institution, separates the economy from society and endangers the latter in the process, it can be expected that, following age-old wisdom and practice, society will generate a countermovement and protect itself against disintegration. Let us look at these two arguments in greater detail.

THE HISTORICAL ARGUMENT

In his treatment of English economic history, Polanyi attaches great importance to the Speedhamland settlement of 1795,[6] which, in one location, guaranteed support for the poor according to a scale depending on the price of bread. Soon copied all over England, the Speedhamland settlement represented traditional Tory collectivism, which recognized "the right to live"[7] by holding society responsible for the lives of all its members. In essence, the Speedhamland law prevented the formation of a free labour market, something which the burgher class, the owners of the newly created industries, greatly desired. According to the theorists of the self-regulating market, hunger and the will to survive should prompt labourers to work in the factories and their wages should be determined by the mechanism of the market. Public support for the poor was seen as an obstable to industrial capitalism.[8]

In 1832 the burgher class gained power in the British parliament, and in 1834 parliament repealed the traditional poor laws. Speedhamland was no longer in force; people no longer enjoyed "the right to live." Because the Poor Law Reform Act of 1834 established the free labour market in England, Polanyi regarded this date as the beginning of modern, industrial capitalism. The self-regulating market was reinforced by subsequent legislation, especially Sir Robert Peel's Bank Act of 1844 and the repeal of the Corn Laws in 1846.[9]

The consequences were devastating and, Polanyi insists, were not confined to the realm of economics. A few revisionist historians have claimed that the poverty of workers in the industrial age represented an improvement over the poverty that had prevailed in villages in pre-industrial time and certainly was not as bad as contemporary authors, for polemical reasons, had claimed. Polanyi regards this argument as misguided. The damage caused by the self-regulating market was above all cultural. By divorcing economic activity from its base in social relations, the free market tore apart the cultural bonds – the values and the inherited institutions – by which people constituted their identity. The new economic system created a devasting *anomie* which seriously damaged the humanity of workers and affected the whole of society and its relation to the natural environment.

It is not out of place to mention that, in the contemporary debate over Third World underdevelopment, political scientists who defend the neo-Marxist "theory of dependency" as well as those who try to refute it present a purely economic analysis of the impact of capitalist development. In fact, however, the dislocation and marginal existence of Third World populations is much better understood with the help of Polanyi's theory that importing Western-style economic development effectively "disembeds" people's economic activity from their social relations, tears the population out of the social matrix that assured their cultural identity, and in the long run destroys their human self-respect. We shall return to this topic in chapter 3.

In England the free, unregulated market system did not remain unchallenged for long. Polanyi shows that from the late 1840s on workers and other people too sought to create their own organizations to protect themselves against the logic of the free market. Eventually Parliament itself introduced law after law to save society and the land from the destructive consequences of the universal market. Polanyi cites a list of government interventions compiled in 1884 by a horror-struck Herbert Spencer, the famous social philosopher, who accused the Liberal Party of having forsaken liberal principles and introduced restrictive legislation. The following is Polanyi's summary of Spencer's list:

In 1860, authority was given to provide "analysts of food and drink out of local rates"; there followed an Act providing "the inspection of gas works"; an extension of the Mines Act "making it penal to employ boys under twelve not attending schools and unable to read and write." In 1861, power was given "to guardians to enforce vaccination"; local boards were authorized "to fix rates of hire for means of conveyance"; and certain locally formed bodies "had given them powers of taxing the locality for rural drainage and irrigation works, and for supplying water to cattle." In 1862, an Act was passed making illegal "a coal-mine with a single shaft"; an Act giving the Council of Medical Education exclusive right "to furnish a Pharmacopoeia, the price of which is to be fixed by the Treasury." … In 1863, came the "extension to compulsory vaccination to Scotland and Ireland." There was also an Act appointing inspectors for the "wholesomeness or unwholesomeness of food"; a Chimney-Sweeper's Act, to prevent the torture and eventual death of children sent to sweep too narrow slots; a Contagious Disease Act; a Public Libraries Act, giving local powers "by which a majority can tax a minority for their books."[10]

What was taking place, according to Polanyi, was the self-organization of society, sometimes with the help of the government and sometimes in spite of it, to protect people and land against the disintegrating forces of the market system. Political democracy made possible the formation of a "civil society" that was distinct from the state, even if in many instances it was assisted by the state. In other words, there arose a complex set of institutions, associations, movements, and networks that enabled people to participate in the shaping of their own social world.

In his interpretation of nineteenth-century England Polanyi reveals himself as a reformist thinker. He has little sympathy for the Marxist theory that in capitalist society the actions of government necessarily aim at protecting the interests of the capitalist class. He rejects the idea that the political order, in this case democracy, is simply a superstructure which reflects power relations defined in economic terms. Polanyi recognizes the reality of the class struggle in England: he admires the collective efforts of workers and ordinary people to set up socialist, cooperative, and labour organizations to defend themselves against the self-regulating market system. But he dismisses the idea that the class struggle by itself is the key for understanding the historical development of society.

The important question for Polanyi is why certain class struggles fail and others succeed. He argues that a class struggle is likely to achieve its goals if it transcends narrowly conceived class interests and promises to protect society as a whole. In that case the class struggle is likely to find support among people of other classes and eventually affect the direction of government policy.

In the context of such reflections, Polanyi offers a carefully worded definition of what he means by the double movement. This definition deserves our attention. "The double movement," Polanyi writes,

> can be personified as the action of two organizing principles in society, each of them setting itself specific institutional aims, having the support of definite social forces and using its own distinctive methods. The one is the principle of economic liberalism, aiming at the establishment of a self-regulating market, relying on the support of the trading classes, and using largely *laissez-faire* and free trade as its method; the other is the principle of social protection aiming at the conservation of man and nature as well as productive organizations, relying on the varying support of those most immediately affected by the deleterious action of the market – primarily, but not exclusively, the working and the landed classes – and using protective legislation, restrictive associations, and other instruments of intervention as its methods.[11]

Here it becomes quite clear that Polanyi is not a functionalist thinker. The counter-movement of protection is not the product of society as such acting according to its own inner logic; it is rather the work of specific groups in society which, relying on their cultural heritage and worried about their material well-being, elect to protect themselves and the society to which they belong. Their effort is not "necessary," not written into the nature of things, but freely chosen and fallible.

The historical experience of nineteenth-century England, Polanyi believes, was repeated in other countries as they moved into industrial capitalism. On this basis he proposes his theory of the double movement. He holds that the conflict between the self-regulating market and civil society is a permanent characteristic of capitalist countries. He also maintains that the self-regulating market and democracy are in the long run irreconcilable. Either the free market economy will give way to a more cooperative, social economy, or, if the free market economy remains in force, it will increasingly depend on authoritarian or even fascist protective rule.

THE ANTHROPOLOGICAL ARGUMENT

Let us now turn to Polanyi's second argument for the double movement, the one based on his anthropological research into the role of the economy in tribal and other pre-modern forms of society. Polanyi shows that throughout history economic activity has been embedded in social relations: economics, in short, was accessary to society. The separation of the economy from society brought about by the self-regulating market goes against the experience of the human race. It reverses the order of things: society becomes accessary to the economy, people and land come to constitute elements of the economic process. Since the constancy of pre-modern economic history reveals the nature of human society, Polanyi argues, we must expect that a society challenged by the self-regulating market will mobilize itself for its own self-protection.

During his career Polanyi became increasingly fascinated by anthropological research. In fact, his greatest contribution to empirical social science was his extensive work on the economics of tribal societies. He believed that tribal societies, because of their simplicity, reveal most clearly the nature of economic activity.

In the simplest societies Polanyi recognizes two types of economic activities which he calls "reciprocity" and "redistribution." Members of tribal societies had symmetrical relations, meaning that the services they rendered were in one form or another reciprocated. People helped one another, relied on one another, gave freely and received freely. But the simple societies also had some sort of central authority capable of providing assistance to the excluded, the hungry, or the sick, thus acting as an agent of redistribution. When someone's dwelling was destroyed, the chief saw to it that the other members of the tribe came to the person's assistance. Reciprocity and redistribution were economic society-building activities. Producing and distributing goods and rendering services were actions that confirmed and stabilized social relations.

A third economic activity, named "householding" by Polanyi, was found in extended families living in relative independence from the tribe. Householding provided most of the goods and services these families required. Extended families were institutions that aimed at a certain self-sufficiency.

Polanyi insists that the early forms of economic life, defined by reciprocity, redistribution, and householding, did not include markets at all. Here he differe from liberal philosophers and economists who assert that human beings have always been, and are by nature, barterers and hagglers, that the local market is therefore the earliest economic institution, and that modern market-capitalism is simply the evolutionary culmination of the simplest form of econonic life. To refute this widely held theory, Polanyi presents an analysis of the genesis and the roles of markets in pre-modern societies.

Historical research uncovers two kinds of markets: the *external* market, which trades in goods brought from distant lands; and the *internal* market, which trades in goods produced in the local communities. These two markets had different origins and functions and were strictly separated. The earliest form of external trade existed for a long time without a competitive market. Because external trade encouraged the use of money, it tended to be concentrated in towns, especially ports, and did not become a universal institution.

By contrast, the internal or local market was competitive from the beginning, involving barter and haggling, yet it did not necessarily presuppose money. People produced for their own needs, but their surplus, that which they did not use, was brought to the market to be exchanged for other goods. This market was controlled to protect the peace of the local community. The exchanges were ritualized and the days and the hours were limited. Local markets were eventually established everywhere. They had the same basic structure, but – Polanyi insists – they did not replace the traditional economic activities of householding, reciprocity, and redistribution. Nor were these markets the starting-point for nation-wide internal trade.

In western Europe, nation-wide internal trade was made possible through the intervention of the state. Polanyi shows that the localism of internal markets was gradually broken down by the mercantilist policies adopted by monarchs. This first took place in England and France. Later it was state power excercised by the successful burgher class that removed traditional barriers, local customs, and inherited community rights to create the free market system.

The structuring of regional markets into a single, independent, self-regulatory market system was not produced by the natural expansion of local markets; it was rather a highly artifical creation, brought about by political power exercised on the social body in response to an equally artificial phenomenon, industrial production in factories. During the industrial revolution, for the first time in history, society became an adjunct of the economic system. No wonder, Polanyi argues, that society defended itself against this process.

On the basis of this examination of Polanyi's historical and anthropological arguments, we may conclude that the theory of the double movement is presented not as a law of history but simply as an historical trend for which there is much evidence. It is clear that Polanyi is neither a functionalist nor a proponent of a dialectical theory of history. He rejects the evolutionary perspective and the idea of necessary progress that in his day dominated social theory on the right and on the left. Polanyi refuses to look upon modernity as the high-point of humankind's historical development. To him it is absurd to interpret the rich variety of traditional cultures simply as stages of preparation for the supposedly higher achievements of the scientific-technological age. He holds that these great cultures embodied profound human wisdom and provided examples of humanity from which we can and should learn today.

At the same time, while rejecting the evolutionary perspective, Polanyi's theory of the double movement provides hope and direction for the future. In the long run, people always seem to be ready to protect themselves and their habitation.

PROTECTING THE ENVIRONMENT

Karl Polanyi was among the first social thinkers to recognize the damaging impact of the self-regulating market upon nature. "What we call land," he writes, "is an element of nature inextricably interwoven with man's institutions. To isolate it and form a market out of it was perhaps the weirdest of all undertakings of our ancestors."[12] At the same time, Polanyi shows that there existed a counter-movement that defended human habitation and sought to protect the land.

Land is part of nature. For the human community, the economic function of land is just one of its many vital purposes. Land is the site of human dwelling, it assures human survival and upholds the community's rootedness in nature, it invests human life with stability, it is the landscape and the seasons. Thus, to make land into a (fictitious) commodity and subject it to the laws of the real estate market threatens to shatter the cultural bases of human existence.

The impact of the commodification of land is seen most clearly in the colonies of the European empires. It is immaterial whether the colonists needed the land because they wanted the metals and resources hidden under it, or whether they needed the land to organize the production of a surplus of food, for in any and every case, Polanyi argues, "the social and cultural system of native life first [had to] be shattered."[13] We see in the colonies a brief, dramatic presentation of what happened in Europe over a longer period of time.

Polanyi describes the stages of this development. It began under feudalism, especially in England, when the aristocracy rationalized and commercialized the treatment of land in order to increase its own revenue. (Such is the historical context of the secularization of church lands.) The process was accelerated with the arrival of industrial capitalism, which made necessary an increase in the production of food and organic raw materials in order to feed and clothe the population in the rapidly growing towns and cities. This stage is best symbolized by the Benthamite reforms in England during the 1830s and 1840s. Bentham had argued that, to create the most favourable conditions for agriculture, it would be necessary to remove traditional rules – entails, unalienable endowments, common lands, tithes, the right of redemption, and so on. For Bentham, this matter was related to individual liberty. To extend that liberty was the aim of a series of acts, such as the Prescription Act and the Inheritance Act, promulgated in the first part of the nineteenth century. Pressure exerted by the burgher class produced similar developments on the European continent, and the end result was the dismantling everywhere of the barriers that had prevented land from being separated from the community.

Linked to all of this was the creation of interregional markets for agricultural products. Because certain industrialized regions with high population density were unable to produce the food they needed, newly created markets brought these products from other regions and eventually from other parts of the world, especially the colonies. This was a new phenomenon. The goods of everyday life had never been bought and sold on a regular basis; until then, grain surpluses had been saved to provision the local neighbourhood, especially the towns, and corn markets had tended to be confined to the region. Now the growth of the metropolis compelled the authorities to loosen restrictions on the corn trade and allow it to develop on a national and eventually world scale.

"The effect of this change," Polanyi writes, "was the true meaning of free trade."[14] The production of goods grown on the land was gradually shifted from the local countryside to the tropical regions, thus extending the division of labour between industry and agriculture to the entire planet. As a result, the peoples of these distant zones were drawn into the vortex of change, the nature of which was obscure to them, and the nations of Europe became dependent upon a system that destroyed their own agricultural population.

But then, from the middle of the nineteenth century on, the counter-movement slowly emerged, offering a social defence against the commodification of the land and the disintegration of local cultures. In the 1870s, Polanyi argues, public legislation in England changed its orientation. The inheritance of the common law was deliberately enhanced by statutes expressly passed to protect the habitations and occupations of the rural classes from the effects of freedom of contract. Efforts were even made to assist the poor by improving their housing and by alloting them land where they could produce food to supplement their diet.

On the continent, Polanyi explains, it was mainly statute law and administrative action that protected peasants and agricultural labourers from the worst effects of urbanization. Since the global division of labour and international trade seriously threatened many rural communities, central European countries were eventually forced to protect their peasant populations through the introduction of corn laws and other tariffs.

That farming was simply "a business" and that those who went broke had to clear out was an idea that frightened not only the peasants but also the landlords. Free trade was their enemy. Yet industrial workers favoured free trade since it reduced the price of food, and so they began to brand the peasantry of the world as reactionaries. Thus, opposed to the protection of the land and rural culture were not only the liberals, who represented the interests of the burghers, but also the revolutionary socialists. City dwellers created the myth that peasants were unintelligent and country life stupid. In central Europe it was eventually the aristocracy and the church that protected the land against the self-regulating real estate market and the peasants against the disintegration of their culture. Through these classes society saved its relationship to nature. This is how Polanyi explains the power exercised by conservative and even reactionary forces in the nations of Europe, long after the advent of democracy and the market economy.

The defence of society's relation to nature is, for Polanyi, one factor explaining the success of European fascism during the 1920s and 1930s, especially in villages and small towns. Despite its dream of conquest and social subordination, fascism was a social movement through which society attempted to protect the land from the "progressive" forces of capitalism and socialism. But because of its commitment to war and slavery, the world – fortunately – turned against fascism and destroyed it.

If Karl Polanyi were still alive today, he would regard the mobilization of people on behalf of ecological causes as part of the counter-movement. He would urge that this mobilization not become ideological, that it not separate itself from existing institutions, that it try to stay close to the popular sector of society, and that it find forms of expression that draw upon the wisdom of the people and their religious and humanistic traditions. Examining environmental destruction in the 1940s, Polanyi emphasized the importance of state power. Territorial sovereignty is so important, he argues, because only through it can society prevent the supply-and-demand mechanism of the market from destroying the natural environment and – in his words – "even its climate … which suffers from the denudation of forests, from erosions and dustbowls, all of which, ultimately, depend upon the land factor."[15] Long before the public outcry against the devastation of the environment, Karl Polanyi was the prophetic theoretician of the ecological movement.

2

The Ethical Foundations of Polanyi's Social Theory

In this chapter I study Karl Polanyi's reflection on the role of ethics in the making of society and in the social scientific understanding of it. Polanyi, who in his personal life was greatly inspired by Leo Tolstoy,[1] was not a philosopher in the strict sense. Yet he believed that as a social and political thinker he had to articulate his intuitions regarding the ethical foundation of human thought and action. He first did so as a young man in the Vienna of the 1920s while struggling against his depression over the useless killing of the Great War. As Polanyi studied social and economic science and became involved in workers' education during these years, he began to ponder the ethical foundations of human existence. His thinking was expressed in two major essays, "Behemoth" and "Über die Freiheit," and in several smaller ones. Because these papers were never published – and because, as Abraham Rotstein has pointed out,[2] Polanyi was to remain faithful throughout his scholarly career to the ethical perspective he had developed in Vienna – I present their argument at some length.[3] Afterwards I turn to an essay written in the 1930s, when Polanyi lived in England. In this essay, entitled "On the Essence of Fascism," Polanyi went so far as to offer a theological argument for his ethical position.

"BEHEMOTH"

In "Behemoth" Polanyi laments the indifference to ethics demonstrated by social and economic science. Scientists have become superstitious, he argues: they believe without evidence that they can understand the shifting patterns of history with the help of clearly defined laws, that on the basis of this knowledge they can make predictions regarding future developments, and that, thus enlightened, they can recommend public policies to those in power. In this approach to social and economic science, Polanyi states, free individuals seem to disappear altogether. Some scientists concede that the ends of social action are determined by ethical considerations – for instance, the protection of society from criminals or the emancipation of industrial workers – but then they insist that the means by which these ends are to be achieved are selected according to purely scientific criteria. Polanyi does not believe in value-free science.

Polanyi's polemic is primarily directed against the scientific Marxism dominant in Austrian socialism, but it also applies to the positivistic social and economic science produced in the liberal tradition. Positivism on the right and on the left, Polanyi argues, recognizes only the external or material dimension of human existence and disregards as historically insignificant human consciousness and human ideals. Even the ends of social action seem no longer freely chosen but rather determined by some sort of necessity, by the human animal's struggle for survival or some other logic implicit in history. Polanyi regarded the consistent exclusion of ethics from social and economic science as one of the factors that prepared the way for European fascism.

Polanyi thought of himself as a man of the left and, as we shall see, proposed what he called a "new socialism." In his Viennese manuscripts he offered a devastating critique of scientific Marxism, especially in its Leninist form. It is worth mentioning, however, that in the 1930s – when Marx's early writings, the *Economic and Philosophical Manuscripts*, suddenly appeared in print – Polanyi (then living in London) discovered the humanistic dimension of Marx's thought and recognized the possibility of an alternative reading of his work.[4]

While still in Vienna, Polanyi defended the ethical foundation of all human knowledge. The first thing we know, he argued, is the experience of being engaged in the day-to-day ethical task of living, the *Lebensweg* as he called it: how to relate ourselves to those dear to us, how to act in regard to our neighbours, how to respond to the culture in which we live, how to assume an appropriate, self-critical attitude towards ourselves. This uninterrupted engagement in the *Lebensweg* was for Polanyi the primary experience of our existence. We are beings of conscience.

The knowledge of the *Lebensweg*, Polanyi continues, allows us to respond to several questions raised by social and economic science. First, is there freedom of the will or do people act out of necesssity? The answer to this question, Polanyi argues, is not a theoretical but an existential one. Why? Because I live every day as one who assumes responsibility for my life. If I do not enjoy this freedom, if I am compelled to act by forces I do not recognize, then I know at least that I desire to be delivered from these forces and choose my *Lebensweg* freely and responsibly.

Secondly, do ideals have historical importance or do they only exist in the mind? For Polanyi, the answer comes again from experience. While the yearning of a single soul achieves very little, he wrote, we know that the yearning of the many affects the course of history. As an example, Polanyi offers "the truths of Jesus," which, by "living in the hearts of millions," have exercised great power through the ages. The content of consciousness, Polanyi insists, may under certain circumstances affect the transformation of material reality.

The third question comes from another angle. Is there being beyond myself? Again Polanyi appeals to the *Lebensweg*. Our ethical conscience demands that we think of others, take into account the consequences of our actions, and assume responsibility with others for the well-being of all. Thus again, ethics is the foundation for our certainty of the world's existence.

In a small, incomplete manuscript from the same period, entitled "Die Lehre vom Lebensweg," Polanyi explored his own ethical understanding of human existence. He believed that the call to live responsibly had been mediated by the founders of the world religion, by great religious personalities, and by men and women of wisdom belonging to all ages, so much so that the human ethical vocation had become inscribed in the major cultural traditions and hence is accessible to ordinary people everywhere. In this regard, Polanyi offered empirical arguments for the universality of the ethical call to love. In his subsequent writings, he proposed that this vocation actually belongs to human nature.

In "Behemoth," Polanyi argues with people of his day who refuse to concede the primacy of the ethical. Some of them, he writes, recognize the call to love, but they believe that social injustice must be overcome before people will be free to love their neighbour. Others, Polanyi writes, commit the opposite error. They claim that the task of living an ethical life and becoming a loving person is so demanding that they must withdraw from social engagement. Though Polanyi has some sympathy for these objections, he forcefully argues against them. The ethical call experienced in the *Lebensweg* affects our relationship to our own small circle and to the larger society to which we belong. There is no double morality, one for the home and the other for the social order. Ethical concern extends to every aspect of human life.

Today, such reflections are commonplace in Christian ethics. But when Polanyi offered these thoughts in the 1920s, there were few ethical thinkers in the churches who shared his convictions.[5] At the time, Polanyi addressed his argument mainly to the Marxist socialists whom he encountered in Vienna. They did not recognize, he thought, the ethical call implicit in human existence. They understood the human impulse to act in purely materialistic terms as an expression of economic class interest, which they regarded as the motor force operative in history. Polanyi was keenly aware that socialist workers struggling to improve the material conditions of their lives were also inspired by high ideals, a desire for social justice and solidarity with the exploited. Yet Marxist theory did not acknowledge this commitment to value and vision but instead interpreted it simply as an expression of collective self-interest.

Polanyi compared the Marxist approach with that of Robert Owen, who envisaged an industrial organization, an alternative to capitalism, based on an ethic of cooperation. What followed after Owen, Polanyi argued, were the cooperatives, the labour movement, and guild socialism, whereas Marx was followed by state capitalism and Lenin's centralized communism. Drawing his inspiration from the British tradition, Polanyi began to speak of the "new socialism," different from Marxism, that must replace the present order.

"ÜBER DIE FREIHEIT"

In a remarkable essay, "Über die Freiheit," Polanyi used his ethical understanding of the human being to produce a rational demonstration in support of the new socialism. To my knowledge, this is an original argument.

How is it, Polanyi begins, that lifeless things like raw materials, merchandise, and machines are able to control so much of human life? Marx, he adds, recognized the enormity of this. Just as people in an earlier period believed that trees and rocks had spirits dwelling within them, so people in the present age believe that material things have a life of their own – like prices going up and down. Is this not the survival of fetishism?

Freedom, Polanyi argues, must mean – among other things – the liberation of people from the domination of impersonal material powers. The new socialism, he continues, reaches beyond the question of justice, that is, the just distribution of society's wealth; it intends to overcome the domination of people by material things and introduce them to a new freedom, the capacity to shape their own society. Socialism is thus concerned with the spiritual dimension of human existence. It is ethical in nature.

Yet socialists, Polanyi goes on, do not need ethical retraining; they do not have to invent a new set of values. The ethical principle developed in the womb of the inherited society retains its full validity. He calls this principle *das bürgerliche Gewissen* – in English, the bourgeois or the citizens' conscience, or possibly simply "the civil conscience." In the feudal order people received their ethical norms from the communities to which they belonged and in which they were embedded: families, villages, guilds, estates, and churches. The Protestant Reformation protested against this ethical conformism in the name of a higher obedience to the scriptural word. But in civil society a new form of ethical awareness emerged, the autonomous conscience, a sense of self-responsibility that would not allow another to set the norms and instead required that persons decide for themselves what is the good and what has to be done. No one can make this decision for the free citizen. Neither the state, nor society, nor the church is an ethical subject. The person alone, ever open to new experiences, new challenges and new evidence, assumes ethical responsiblity for his or her *Lebensweg*.

Living in civil society, a person is inevitably co-responsible for what happens in it. The class division, for instance, which unjustly assigns one sector of the population to subservience, is not a process from which an individual can remain aloof but one in which he or she inevitably participates. In a simpler society, Polanyi argues, people knew the impact their actions had on others: they knew the farmer, the miller, the baker, and the other craftsmen and merchants with whom they dealt. They could estimate whether their interaction with them was just or unjust. Their society was "transparent." But, because of ever increasing complexity, modern, industrial society has become largely "opaque." We realize that our actions have an impact on other people, but most of the time we do not know what this impact is. We are aware that our participation in society makes us co-responsible for the good and for the evil done by society, but we do not know with any precision what these good and evil actions are.

In this situation, Polanyi argues, the civil conscience is deeply anguished. People desire to be ethical and assume responsiblity for the consequences of what they do, but in an opaque society they cannot know what these consequences are. The cup of coffee we drink in the morning – to take a simple example – raises an uncomfortable question regarding the impact of the coffee trade on the coffee pickers and their tropical villages. Complex society leaves us largely ignorant. The ethical longing of the bourgeois, Polanyi argues, cannnot be satisfied within bourgeois society.

How have people responded to this anguish? Immanuel Kant, according to Polanyi, made a desparate attempt to escape the dilemma by defining personal self-responsibility in terms of an empty categorical imperative in which the neighbour disappeared completely. Kant created a notion of duty to principle that remained indifferent to the consequences of the action taken. According to Max Weber, many Christians in the Protestant tradition resonated with such a *Gewissensethik* (ethics of conscience), which tended to restrict the significant ethical decisions to the extra-societal aspects of life, that is, those dealing with inwardness, intimacy, and transcendence.

Yet the great majority of citizens escape the dilemma in a different way. With Max Weber, Polanyi holds that most people prefer to follow a half-hearted ethic, one that does not challenge the whole of their existence. He also remarks that the fascists of his day cynically repudiated the civil conscience altogether.

This, then, is Polanyi's original argument: the longing of the bourgeois conscience transcends the possibilities of bourgeois society. What this conscience calls for is the creation of a transparent society that allows its members to estimate the effects of what they are doing and thus assume ethical responsibility for their actions. Civil society, that is to say, the capitalist society to which we belong, is dominated by material forces that behave according to a logic of their own and thus deprive the citizens of the responsibility for their social life. The new socialism, the society demanded by the ethical conscience, will offer people what Polanyi called *gesellschaftliche Freiheit* or, in English, social freedom – the freedom to be ethical under the conditions of industrial society.

Polanyi's concept of freedom, we notice, is not a liberal one: for him, freedom is not the capacity to choose and do as one pleases. Freedom, rather, is always the capacity to live an ethical life. He distinguishes between *personal* and *collective* freedom. The latter freedom, not enjoyed under present conditions, only becomes available when people have been liberated from the opaque forces that now determine their lives.

Implicit in the notion of collective freedom is a double intuition regarding the nature of society. Polanyi presupposes that there is no human action that does not have some social consequences, and, conversely, that there is no power structure in society that does not rest in some way on the behaviour of individuals. This second affirmation stands against any mechanistic or structuralist understanding of society. According to Polanyi, there are no fixed laws that define the life of society. If it seems to people that such laws do exist, then the reason for this is that they have been successfully persuaded to see society in that way. What people must discover is that the structures in which they live rest upon their own participation and that, if they so wished, if there existed a collective will, they could actually transform these structures. Against the structuralist tendency in sociology, Polanyi puts the emphasis on agency.[6] The subject of history is responsible human beings.

Polanyi consistently rejects the notion of economic laws, whether they be proposed by liberals or Marxists. Humans are free, at least in principle, to create the economy they consider just and humane. Striving for "transparency" in the complex social conditions of today is not pursuing an impossible dream, not an ideal that can never be realized. For Polanyi, transparency is a possible utopia, a state of affairs that should be the object of a social struggle, even if this struggle never comes to an end.

In "Über die Freiheit" Polanyi makes remarks about human existence that are important for the understanding of his entire intellectual achievement. He has a keen sense of the anguish that grips members of modern society. A part of us, he argues, contributes to the cause of the injustices committed by society, while another part of us, separated from the first and possibly unaware of it, is the effect of these unjust conditions. These two parts stand against each another, they divide the soul, they cannot be synthesized, they produce internal division and ethical dilemma. The social conditions in which we live make us colonizer and colonized at the same time. Few ethicists have recognized the human condition thus.

From our anguish comes the longing for *collective* freedom. Yet, because Marxist socialism has paid so little attention to the individual person, Polanyi insists that, even in a society gifted with collective freedom, *personal* freedom remains unremittingly important and retains its independent identity. As Polanyi puts it (in my own translation): "The greater and in fact the essential part of human life takes place in the extra-societal sphere. A person's relationship to the world around him, his friends, his family, his life's companion and his children, his relation to his own capacities and his work, his relation to himself: the honesty with which he critically encounters himself and the response he gives in his innermost heart to his own existence marked by mortality. Here the personal freedom comes to life through which a human being become truly human. Without this freedom, a human society is unthinkable."

Polanyi's understanding of modern society made him aware of the degree of ignorance in which we live. And, because he realized that we can never be certain that our actions will have the consequences we anticipate, his ethical passion, according to Abraham Rotstein, was tamed by a certain caution or reserve.[7] Polanyi's intellectual approach did not allow him to become a revolutionary. He was a passionate reformist.

"THE ESSENCE OF FASCISM"

When Polanyi moved to England in the early 1930s, he found a hearing in the labour movement and, more especially, among Christian socialists. Eventually he involved himself again in the education of workers. After 1933, the year Hitler assumed power in Germany, Polanyi produced an essay on the nature of fascism,[8] in which he used his acquaintance with the continental situation to explain to British workers the threat of the Nazi movement. He argued that Italian and Austrian fascism was mild compared with the German fascism of the Nazi Party: it was in that party that fascism revealed its essence, its profound opposition to humanism, its philosophy and brutal practice of inequality.

Polanyi shows that fascism regards the ethical conscience of the individual as the principal enemy which it, fascism, must destroy if it wants to be victorious. In "Über die Freiheit" he had used the term "civil conscience"; however, in the essay now under review, he adopts a curious vocabulary: he calls the civil conscience "individualism." He does so, I presume, because an Austrian fascist thinker whom he quotes at length lauds the historical role of collectivism and defines fascist philosophy as anti-individualism. The thesis of Polanyi's essay is that German fascism, faithful to its philosophical essence, aims at the destruction of the workers' movement and Christianity, the two loci where the individual ethical conscience is most alive.

Confronted with Nazism, Polanyi feels that it is necessary to locate the origin of the civil conscience in the religious traditions, in particular in Christianity. He had hinted at this relationship before, and now he makes it explicit, claiming that Christian faith is the most solid ground for ethical conviction. Given that he was writing in the 1930s, his praise of Christianity is surprising. Polanyi is keenly aware of the influence of the so-called German Christians (Christians committed to Nazism) on the Protestant Church of Germany, and he mentions the complicity of the Catholic Church in several countries with reactionary politics and sometimes even with fascist parties. Yet he is convinced that the roots of the Western moral conscience lie in the Christian tradition, and that this spiritual heritage has not totally disappeared. He mentions Christians in Austria and Germany who disagreed with their ecclesiastical leaders and stood up for socialist justice, and he reports a recent development, the resistance to Hitler's dictatorship by a group of Christians in Germany. He further maintains that the Nazis, in their fight against the socialist movement and its ethical inspiration, cannot in the long run avoid opposing what he calls the teaching of Jesus. By virtue of its essence, fascism must inevitably turn against the churches. There is evidence, Polanyi claims, that this is already beginning in Germany.

To clarify the nature of the Christian conscience and the ethical inspiration of socialism, Polanyi introduces – rather polemically – the distinction between "atheistic" and "Christian" individualism. The atheist conscience rejects any relation to an absolute and for this reason, possibly without intending it, affirms itself as the absolute measure. Polanyi turns to the novels of Dostoyevsky for examples of typical atheist individualists. In *The Demons*, Kiriloff exclaims, "If there is no God, then I, Kiriloff, am God." Polanyi find this reasoning convincing. God, he writes, is that which gives meaning to human life and creates the difference between good and evil. If there exists no such God, then I am forced to do these things myself and thus become my own God. In *The Demons*, Kiriloff pursues the full realization of his divinity by wrestling with and eventually overcoming his fear of death. He wins this battle as he commits suicide. In all of his novels, Polanyi tells us, Dostoyevsky uncovers the nature and the limitations of the self-sufficient personality.

Polanyi continues his argument against more recent poets and philosophers who have adopted the self-sufficient person as their ideal. Their individualism, he laments, undermines the virtues of justice and solidarity, which are absolutely necessary for the creation of a non-exploitative society.

This presentation of "atheist individualism" is undoubtedly polemical. When speaking of the "civil conscience" in his earlier writings, Polanyi had not described it as necessarily theistic. All he proposed at that time was that the notion of the autonomous, self-responsible person was ultimately rooted in the great religious traditions, especially Christianity. But, confronted by the threat of German fascism, he comes to believe that the individual conscience can be protected only if it is religiously grounded.

Allow me to add that the heroic-tragic atheism of Kiriloff does not, in my opinion, represent the atheism so widespread in contemporary culture. What we have today, it seems to me, is the "secular atheism" of people in whose mental universe the God-question has never seriously emerged: some of them live lives of self-gratification, while others identify themselves with an ethical tradition and live in accordance with its values. There is also the "religious atheism" of those who want to believe in God but find themselves unable to do so because of the massive, never-ending suffering experienced by people throughout history, suffering to which God seems indifferent.

In his essay on the nature of fascism, Polanyi contrasts heroic-tragic individualism with Christian individualism, defined by a contrary relation to the absolute. Here the individual person has infinite value because there is God. Christians find themselves surrounded by other people whom they honour, whose infinite dignity they recognize, whom they embrace as their brothers and sisters and for whose well-being they feel morally responsible. To say that people have souls, Polanyi writes, is another way of affirming that they deserve infinite respect, are equal among themselves, belong to one another, and constitute a single human family bound together in solidarity. This, according to Polanyi, is the teaching of Jesus. Christian individualism is thus essentially social.

In another context, Polanyi recalls that in the nineteenth century Robert Owen, whose social vision he greatly admires, abandoned the Christian faith because he believed that the teaching of Jesus called for a narrow individualism focused on personal salvation and otherworldy piety.[9] Polanyi believes that Owen was wrong on this issue. Similarly, through conversations with members of the Christian Left in England,

Polanyi had learnt that many of them also had the impression that the teaching of Jesus contained no social message and that they were thus obliged to draw their social inspiration from other sources. In his essay on fascism, he endeavours to persuade them otherwise.

There does exist, Polanyi argues, a Christian concept of society. What the New Testament reveals is that persons belong to a community of men and women whom they love, for whom they are co-responsible, and with whom they must create a common world. The society they build together must never be allowed to humiliate or damage the dignity of any one of its members. Polanyi writes that the discovery of the soul is at the same time the discovery of society. Society, seen from his perspective, is a "relationship of persons."

Many sociological theories, following Emile Durkheim, recognize that individual persons come to be through interaction with others and that, in this sense, society does not remain purely extrinsic to persons but actually enters into the definition of their identity. Persons are persons-in-community. Reflecting on the communal nature of human beings, a number of twentieth-century Christian philosophers, among them John Macmurray,[10] proposed an ethical social theory called "personalism"[11] which tried to bridge and transcend the individualism of the liberal tradition and the collectivism of scientific Marxism. John Macmurray was a Christian socialist thinker in Great Britain with whom Polanyi was acquainted and to whom he refers with approval in his essay on fascism. When Polanyi writes that the discovery of the soul is at the same time the discovery of society or that society is a relationship of persons, he offers a personalist conception of society, that is, a society characterized by cooperation and co-responsibility that recognizes the personal dignity and equality of its citizens.

Implicit in Polany's concept of society is a critique of societies that structure people in inequality, distribute unjustly wealth, power, and prestige, and remain subservient to opaque forces that prevent people from understanding the ethical implications of their actions. Society is meant to be just and transparent. Polanyi believes that basic Christian teaching reveals the true nature of society and implicit in that teaching is the ethical summons to reform accordingly the existing social structures. In his essay on fascism, I conclude, Polanyi offers an ethical theory based on what in classical philosophy and theology is called "natural law," except that for him this "law" is made known in the teaching of Jesus.

Polanyi claims that, for St Augustine, the New Testament concept of a society created by relationships of love and free from injustice and oppression is an ideal that can be realized only in small communities. The "city of God," defined by love of God and neighbour, would always remain a minority community in the wider society; the latter would inevitably be the "city of men," characterized by self-seeking and personal ambition. But since the days of Augustine, Polanyi argues, we have learnt that even societies are transformable. The collapse of the Roman empire was followed by the creation of the feudal order, and the feudal order was succeeded by civil society. According to Polanyi, as we have seen, civil society has a built-in principle of transformation: it expects its citizens to act according to their conscience. This ethical conscience cannot rest until society becomes transparent, just, and participatory. Finally, because fascism sought to destroy individualism, Polanyi argues that the labour movement, the socialist parties, and the Christian churches must stand together and resist it as their mortal enemy.

Living in England in the 1930s, Polanyi, as I mentioned above, read and was greatly impressed by the recently published early writings of Karl Marx. In those writings Marx showed that he also understood the essence of society as a set of transparent interpersonal relations that frees people from the alienation inflicted by an exploitative order. Polanyi, for his part, argues that Christians can use Marx's analysis of capitalism even while remaining wary of his philosophy, which sees the human as wholly immanent in society. Faithful to his basic understanding of the personal *Lebensweg*, Polanyi responds to Marx by positing the concept of a vast extra-societal sphere in which human beings constitute their lives. Marx offers no ethical guidance, Polanyi writes, on how people should live once socialism has been realized, nor – one might add – on how people should behave as they struggle for their political objectives in a socialist party.

I do not know how important theological reflections were for Karl Polanyi in subsequent years. Yet he always retained his ethical perspective. While struggling against a monstrous danger such as German fascism, people are often prompted to seek metaphysical or even religious foundations for their resistance. In the process, they sometimes have profound spiritual experiences. But in many cases, once these great dangers subside, the sense of urgency is diffused and what was important or even crucial at one time becomes simply a memory. Many intellectuals who in the 1980s struggled against communist regimes in eastern Europe and found great strength in their identification with the Christian tradition became increasingly indifferent to the message of religion as these dictatorships collapsed. I have no idea whether and to what extent Karl Polanyi regarded himself as a believing Christian all of his life – and, in any case, this is none of my business. What remained constant was his ethical vision and his esteem for religion.

THE REALITY OF SOCIETY

"The discovery of society" and "the reality of society" are rich concepts in Polanyi's writings – he also uses them in the last chapter of *The Great Transformation* – though he never offers a complete definition of what he means by these terms.[12] In the essay on the nature of fascism, the "reality of society" refers to the hidden, ethical content of society that must be revealed. Just as persons have a nature which they must discover and to which they must learn to be faithful, so society too has a nature which must be understood and which generates a summons for social change. The discovery of the person or the soul is rooted in the religious tradition, but the discovery of society in the full sense, Polanyi holds, took place only in modern times when people became critical of the existing orders and recognized that they could be transformed. Understanding society also means becoming aware that the market and the state are not the only realities and that the subjectivity at the base – in the form of people's multiple interactions – is the most powerful source for social transformation. Encountering society as an ethical, interactive reality engenders a commitment to modesty and self-limitation so that space is left for other societies, resources are saved for future generations, and the natural environment is rescued from destruction.

Polanyi was not a philosopher, nor was he a theologian. But he had profound intuitions of philosophical and theological ideas that in subsequent decades were to acquire great importance in the reflections of the Christian churches, such as the documents of the World Council of Churches and the social teachings of Pope John Paul II. Today the pope proposes that human beings are free agents or "subjects" responsible for their lives and the institutions to which they belong. A society deserves to be called just, John Paul II argues, to the extent that it acknowledges "the subjectivity" of its members, that is to say, the free exercise of their co-responsibility for the well-being of all.[13] It is thus no exaggeration to say that Karl Polanyi's thoughts on ethics anticipated developments that were to take place in the Christian churches at a later time.

The reality of society as Polanyi perceived it also implied that the scientific effort to understand a social situation was also and at the same time an ethical task. Again, Polanyi did not develop this point in a systematic way. Yet, as I pointed out in my examination of *The Great Transformation* in chapter 1, Polanyi's scientific approach was guided by an ethical commitment. Social science has an objective dimension, contained in the demonstration of a thesis through a systematic alignment of facts, but it also has a subjective dimension that is present in the vision and values held by the researcher. Social-scientific research is always undertaken from a particular perspective or standpoint, always makes use of paradigms or concepts that inevitably have value-implications, and is always guided by an intention to answer certain questions and achieve certain goals. Whether the scientist realizes it or not, social-scientific research is a form of social action; it may have the effect of stabilizing the existing order or supporting movements for social change, but in both cases it has consequences for society. Though positivistic practitioners of social and economic science claim maximum objectivity and deny the subjective dimension, it is generally recognized that the important controversies in the social sciences cannot be resolved by the scientific method alone and indeed reflect profound differences in philosophical presuppositions.

Analysing the presuppositions operative in Polanyi's work would be a study in itself. Yet it is possible to offer some thoughts on the underlying assumptions of his work: on the perspective adopted by him, on the value-implications of the concepts he used, and on the intentions that guided his research.

As a socialist of sorts, engaged in workers' education and impressed by the ethical imperative present in life itself, Polanyi studied the crisis of our times from a perspective of solidarity with the vulnerable and exploited. He focused not on the remarkable achievements of the industrial revolution but on the effects of this revolution upon the ordinary people and their environment. His standpoint was that of the Left. We have already seen, moreover, that Polanyi rejected the concept – basic to utilitarianism and mainstream economics – that human beings are defined by the struggle for self-preservation and self-promotion. He did not see humans as "utility maximizers" whose lives are determined by necessity. Rather, he held that humans have a spiritual dimension, are gifted with personal freedom, and act from a variety of motives, including material self-interest as well as social solidarity and a desire to protect their habitation. Polanyi looked upon humans as cultural and ethical beings. Even his concept of society, as we noted earlier, was an ethical one.

Finally, Polanyi's intention in writing *The Great Transformation* was to offer a scientific demonstration for his thesis of the double movement in capitalist society. He was convinced that, by re-reading the historical evidence, interpreting more deeply human suffering, and presenting the data in systematic form, he would lend support to the counter-movement and thereby promote a culture of hope in difficult times.

3
Polanyi's Contemporary Relevance

Since the 1960s, social ethics has assumed increasing importance in the theological education, pastoral practice, and ministry of the Christian churches. One of the reasons for this development is the recognition that in the past the churches tended to identify themselves, consciously or unconsciously, with the societies in which they lived and, more especially, with the ruling powers or dominant ideologies. Although individual Christians and critical Christian movements gave prophetic witness in their societies, the churches as a whole tended to remain silent in the face of the injustices practised by their societies. Today, their behaviour is much different.

But to adopt critical positions on social issues, Christian social ethics must be in dialogue with the social, economic, and political sciences. Some Christians have denied this. They believe that the Scriptures themselves are so rich in meaningful stories and ethical teaching – for instance, the exodus, the covenant made with Israel, the exile of the people, their eventual return and the founding of the church – that by relying on them alone the churches are able to formulate their social message. Yet the work done by theologians who adopt this viewpoint clearly reveals that they read the Scriptures with presuppositions taken from their own world and from the social theories belonging to their culture.[1] There is no escape from one's contemporary self-understanding. Even in reading the Bible, we bring to the text perceptions of society that belong to our time.

The two preceding chapters revealed that several of Polanyi's positions have an affinity with Christian social thought. What concerns me in this chapter is the light Polanyi's social analysis sheds on the present situation.

When Ronald Reagan and Margaret Thatcher, with support from the capitalist élite, abandoned the Keynesian capitalism that had prevailed since the Second World War and adopted monetarist economic policies, the economy gradually returned to the practices of the self-regulating market system, this time on a global scale. As a result, society has experienced profound transformations. We suffer from massive unemployment, growing poverty, increasing social insecurity, cultural disintegration, and the marginalization of ever larger sectors of the population, including youth. Karl Polanyi helps us to analyse the damage done by the self-regulating market system, but has his theory of the double movement any validity today?

To deal with Polanyi's contemporary relevance I will, in the first part of this chapter, explore certain of his ideas that help us to understand the human predicament and uncover the still unrealized possibilities of the present. In the second part I will examine whether there are counter-movements in modern society.

EXPLORING POLANYI'S PROPOSAL

The Dialectic of the Enlightenment

Polanyi rejected the evolutionary perspective and the idea of necessary progress. He did not believe that human history moved through various stages to an ultimate fulfilment; he refused to look upon the rich and varied cultures of antiquity as preparations for the supposedly more perfect society of modern times and he lamented the fact that modern society increasingly relied upon instrumental rationality and dismissed reflections on ethics and values as unscientific. In contrast, he thought that the ancients showed great wisdom in the organization of their communities, a wisdom from which we could and should learn in our present situation.

Still, Polanyi did not repudiate the Enlightenment altogether. As we have noted, he greatly treasured the emergence of the "bourgeois" or "civil" conscience, that is, the autonomous conscience of the person who recognizes himself or herself as a responsible agent. This ethical achievement was the product of the Enlightenment in its early stages, before it allowed itself to be taken over by instrumental rationality. It seems to me, therefore, that Polanyi's view of the Enlightenment can be fitted into the intellectual framework of the Frankfurt School philosophers who criticized the Enlightenment without totally disavowing it.[2]

Originally, according to the Frankfurt School, Enlightenment rationality had two dimensions: "instrumental" or scientific-technological reason, and "practical or ethical reason." Yet, because of the success of industrial capitalism, the advance of science, and the wealth produced by the burgher class, instrumental reason came to be seen as the only valid form of knowing and ethical reflections were increasingly regarded as "soft," non-rational, a matter of feeling. Once deprived of its ethical dimension, the spirit of the Enlightenment promoted a purely instrumental view of human beings and their natural environment and thus actually constituted an obstacle to the humanization of society. But, at the same time, those in the Frankfurt School were afraid that turning one's back on the spirit of modernity would endanger the heritage of human rights, the

Enlightenment's great achievement. What they adocated, therefore, was the "dialectical negation" of the Enlightenment, a term that referred to a twofold intellectual exercise: first, the critique and de-centring of instrumental reason and the rejection of scientism; and second, the retrieval of the ethical dimension originally associated with the Enlightenment. Polanyi's work fits well into this framework of "critique" and "retrieval."

For Polanyi, as we have explained, the destructive aspect of modern society was the self-regulating market system, introduced in society by state power, which created isolated, competitive individuals and undermined the bonds of social solidarity, the matrix of human well-being. Polanyi showed how unfettered capitalism disembedded people's economic activities from their social relations and led to widespread rootlessness, loss of identity, and spiritual anomie. Polanyi recognized a curious contradiction in the market system. On the one hand, the system depended for its efficient operation upon many cultural (non-market) factors: virtues such as honesty, trust, diligence, and responsibility and support groups such as families, neighbourhoods, and communities. On the other hand, the market system undermined these cultural factors inherited from tradition and introduced fragmentation and instability.

Still, Polanyi rejected neither markets nor industrialization. What he expected was that the emergence of a countermovement in industrial society would lead to a retrieval of a sense of social solidarity and create societal conditions in which markets and industries serve, rather than destroy, human community.

Liberation Theology

Let me at this point say a few words about the contribution Polanyi's social theory could make to Latin American liberation theology. It is well known that this theology, as originally formulated, made use of a neo-Marxist social theory to demonstrate that the situation of Latin American societies at the edge of the capitalist system had led to an increase in their material poverty. This was the famous "dependency theory," first articulated by André Gunder Frank and later reformed and refined by Latin American social scientists.[3] In recent years, dependency theory has been criticized by many economists, even by some in sympathy with Latin American liberation. They have argued, for instance, that some economically dependent societies actually experience economic development. Questioning the validity of dependency theory has created confusion among Latin American theologians.

Karl Polanyi's social analysis offers a better understanding of the Latin American experience. This innovative scholar made the bold assertion that material poverty in itself is not a tragic event if people are integrated in a community with survival skills and a strong sense of solidarity. That is how the great majority of people have lived throughout history. But material poverty is tragic if people are *not* integrated into such a community: then their material poverty is accompanied by humiliation, the loss of self-respect, and an entry into self-destruction. Such is the poverty in the urban slums of North America and such the deprivation of the dislocated and marginalized populations of Latin America.

According to Polanyi, we recall, the institution of industrial capitalism forced people into economic activities that were disembedded from their social relations: this undermined the cultural matrix out of which the people defined their personal identity. Polanyi demonstrated that the identity-destroying poverty existing in the industrialized parts of nineteenth-century Europe was exported to other continents whenever and wherever the Western mode of production and distribution was introduced. It is unimportant, therefore, whether the economic dependency theory is correct or not. What Polanyi denounced was the devastating human impact of the self-regulating market system on traditional communities, even if they should experience some economic growth. The poverty Polanyi studied and measured was not principally the economic one, but rather the isolation, depression, and cultural debasement produced by the separation of work from people's social relations.

The reliance on neo-Marxist dependency theory, it is worth mentioning, did not prompt liberation theology to lose its focus on the social and ethical dimensions of human existence. Liberation theology did not endorse the Western evolutionary ideal, be it Marxist or liberal. Latin American radicalism saw itself as an anti-development movement. It looked forward to a society where the economy, freed from the power of foreign and local capital, satisfied the economic and social needs of the population. In such an economy, all members of society would be involved in production, production would aim primarily at satisfying the needs of the population, the resources used would principally be those available in the region, and the technology employed would be appropriate to people's skills. The liberationists believed that a society focused on subsistence and transparent human relations was possible in Latin America because *homo œconomicus* had not yet arrived among the Latin American masses – the communitarian spirit of Latin American culture had not yet been invaded by Western, self-interested individualism. The liberation theologians hoped that just as – according to Max Weber – early (pre-industrial) capitalism spread rapidly in Europe because of the "Protestant ethic," so populist socialism supported by the liberation movements would find wide acceptance in Latin America owing to the "Catholic ethic" that was still strong among the people.

The attempt to realize this dream in Nicaragua was undermined by American pressure. A decade or two later, that *kairos*, that special moment of history, is past. At present, the Westernization of Latin American is in full swing, with ever greater sectors of the population pushed to the margin of society.

The Discovery of Society

Though Polanyi was a severe critic of the self-regulating market system, he also opposed the idea that the state alone should have the power to regulate the economy. Polanyi believed that markets are necessary institutions in modern society. Even in the early 1920s, as we noted above, he rejected the communism of the Soviet Union and argued against the Marxist thinkers who wanted to abolish markets and put the government in charge of the economy. From the 1930s on, contending with fascism, Polanyi supported social-democratic policies and governments, but he did not put his trust in political struggles alone. For him, the problems of the economy were social rather than political, and hence they had to be solved through social and cultural transformation. State power on its own could not do it.

In an interesting article in line with Polanyi's logic, Jacques Godbout has shown that the state can also become disembedded from society.[4] This happens when the state, without respecting communities and listening to citizens, imposes its own governing logic from above to the detriment of the social fabric and the vitality of society. Godbout speaks of the "self-regulating state." Polanyi himself realized that the welfare state has its dark side. He expected society to support its members in need of help, but he criticized the bureaucratic welfare state because it supplied material help without creating community and in many cases even pushed the poor into greater isolation.

If neither the market nor the state have the answer to the problems of modern society, where then can it be found? For

Polanyi, the key word was society. We noted earlier that he spoke of the "discovery of society" as an important event in modern times, even if he never clearly explained the rich meaning which he gave this phrase. Since society was so complex, human actions in society were always accompanied by unexpected consequences; in short, society was opaque and ambiguous. At the same time, Polanyi believed that society had a substantive reality that generated energy for social change. Thus he looked upon society as the matrix of the counter-movement. People living in communities and organized at the grassroots were capable of resisting the forces of the market or of the state which threatened to undo their habitation. Polanyi held that society was essentially a relationship among persons and that, whenever this relationship was reified or subjected to external forces, people experienced an inner summons to become active in social transformation. Discovering society meant all these things for Polanyi. In this regard he anticipated what later sociologists studying social movements would call "civil society."

Beyond "Homo Œconomicus"

We mentioned above that Polanyi rejected the concept of *homo œconomicus.* Humans were not "utility-maximizers." In his anthropological studies, Polanyi demonstrated that people's economic activities were never simply economic: they also fulfilled cultural and social functions. It was only in modern market societies that self-preservation and self-promotion tended to become the overriding motive for people's actions. People thought they had to define themselves through their struggle to improve their material conditions. What emerged as a result was a new selfishness and a new loneliness. But this materialistic self-preoccupation was itself a collective creation, the cultural product of a particular economic system.

Classical economics assumed the validity of *homo œconomicus*: because people were seen as "utility maximizers," their behaviour was believed to be predictable. Today, since utility can be expressed in quantitative terms, mainstream economists look upon their discipline as an exact science. It is possible, they believe, to discover the laws operative in the economy, to predict what will happen in the future, and to specify the short- and long-range consequences of changes in the organization of the economy.

Polanyi was an economist who did not regard economics as an exact science. Recognizing the cultural and social dimension in people's economic activities – their daily work, their buying and trading, their saving, their consumption – he attempted to "transcend economic categories in favour of sociological ones."[5] For instance, instead of characterizing poverty in terms of exploitation, loss of income, or absence of funds, he preferred – as we have seen – to render an account of it in terms of social dislocation, cultural debasement, or loss of self-respect.

Polanyi adopted a new approach to the study of the economy. Instead of looking exclusively at the "formal economy," that is, the economic activity instituted for profit making, he recognized the "substantive economy." By this term he meant all instituted economic activities – whether part of the "formal" economy or the "informal" one – resulting in the production and distribution of material goods. While mainstream economics studies almost exclusively the formal economy that is recorded and constitutes the gross national product, Polanyi also investigated the traditional economic activities surviving in modern society: forms of redistribution, customs of reciprocity, householding, forums of non-profit exchange as well as unrecorded, small-scale production. Polanyi argued that without this informal economy, without the hundreds of little services people render to one another in the family, among friends, and in neighbourhoods, society could not survive.

Since this informal economy is embedded in social relations, it differs from the formal economy and could possibly heal some of the isolation and fragmentation caused by the market system. There are, then, social and not only economic reasons why Polanyi thought that the informal economy should be promoted.

For Polanyi, humans were cultural beings. He admired traditional societies where the work people did and their dreams of the future were integrated in the community to which they belonged. For this reason, he lamented the social disintegration produced by the self-regulating market system. People now worked for themselves and entertained purely private dreams. Polanyi denounced the mass media, which, through the power of public opinion, made people increasingly self-concerned, left them little space for critical thinking, and undermined the cultural sources of social solidarity.

The Western system makes people shiftless. The market-driven culture continually increases people's needs and wishes and prompts them to see themselves as lacking what they desire and thus in some sense as disadvantaged. Of course, the Western system provides many of these needs, but it does so in a totally impersonal manner, leaving people as aloof and isolated as they were before. Polanyi recognized that even the modern welfare state redistributes public wealth in a purely bureaucratic manner and is unable to rescue people from their anomie. As Marguerite Mendell has pointed out,[6] Polanyi did not believe that thinking about human beings in terms of their needs, even their basic needs, was fruitful. Whereas that approach sees people as beings who by nature are always lacking something, Polanyi preferred to look upon people as creators capable of inventing the culture that would sustain them.

For the same reason, Polanyi, who analysed in detail the oppressive impact of the Western economic system, did not like to refer to people as "victims" or as "oppressed." Even under oppressive conditions, he believed, people often retain their human potential to innovate and protect their community.

It is important to add at this point that Polanyi was not nostalgic about the past. He was not a conservative who wished to protect traditional societies from social change. He realized that traditional cultures contained structures of domination that placed heavy burdens on certain sectors of the population and demanded ritual conformity that did not allow the maturing of conscience and the entry into the fullness of the human vocation – goals which Polanyi had no hesitation in describing as basic to human nature. To the extent that traditional societies sustained patterns of inequality, they too lacked transparency, they too failed to be *relationships* among persons in the strong sense Polanyi gave to this word. Though this innovative social thinker had a rather conventional view of the role of women in society, his demand for transparency, equality, and co-responsibility had an implicit feminist thrust which he himself did not explore.

Polanyi recognized the impact on people's self-understanding exerted by mainstream culture and the dominant institutions, but he did not think that people are wholly defined by the system to which they belonged. Even in modern, capitalistic society, people are not totally determined by economic motivations. In their daily lives, they still practise love, friendship, and solidarity.[7] People at the community level, Polanyi believed, remain capable of responding in imaginative ways to protect their communities and the natural environment. He rejected the presupposition entertained by liberals and Marxists that people never act on behalf of the common good or the whole of society. Since people's identity is socially defined, Polanyi insisted that people are often willing to make great sacrifices to protect the communal matrix to which they belong. He saw in that willingness the root of the counter-movement.

Writing against fascism in the 1930s, Polanyi had recognized that the fascist movement was a violent reaction not only against unemployment and material poverty but also against the social disintegration and loss of identity produced by the free market system. Fascism was the return of the "repressed" in perverted form, the forging of the social bond dissolved by liberalism and Marxism. In fascism, people willingly defined their collectivity in terms that supressed their own personal freedom and repudiated the human dignity of outsiders. Fascism had to be fought. But it was Polanyi's hope at that time that through the struggle against fascism industrial society would become more democratic, by which he meant more open to participation and more supportive of social movements at the community level.

Re-embedding the Economy

Since, for Polanyi, the principal vice of the self-regulating market system was its disembedding of the economy from the social relations that constitute society, we must ask whether he believed it was possible to "re-embed" economic activity in a complex, industrial society such as ours. Polanyi held that his idea of a participatory, decentralized industrial economy that created rather than undermined social relations was not totally new. In the nineteenth century Robert Owen had created an alternative model of industrialization and envisaged the organization of society as a federation of cooperative towns and villages. Later, British guild socialism had advocated the democratization of the economy through worker-owned industries, credit unions, and community-based companies.

In his early essay "Behemoth," Polanyi mentioned with approval that certain guild socialists divided the goods society needed into three kinds: first, personal goods such as food, clothing, and housing; second, goods for the town such as streets, buildings, tramways, and parks; and third, goods for the entire society such as trains, airplanes, broadcasting, and postal service. The first two kinds of goods, these guild socialists proposed, could be produced by the local or regional economy; only the third kind demanded large-scale companies on the national or international level. This represented the guild-socialist approach to decentralization.

Later, in his anthropological studies, Polanyi demonstrated – as we saw chapter 1 – that in simple societies economic activity was made up of householding, reciprocity, redistribution, and exchange. These activities exercised a community-creating function. By contrast, in today's complex society the highly formalized monetary exchange taking place in the market system – including the exchange of labour for wages – has become the principal economic activity. It is wholly quantified, depersonalized to the extreme, and no longer generates community. Economic activity in the welfare state also includes the redistribution of wealth, yet this tends to take place in bureaucratic fashion and hence fails to create personal relations. The informal economy remains largely hidden and underdeveloped.

If economic activity in an industrial society is again to be embedded in people's social relations, it must promote the cooperative principle at every level of industrial production and foster the informal economy, including local cooperative activity and householding. Small-scale production of food, clothes, and furniture at home or on a cooperative basis among friends or neighbours and the provision of services by community-supported groups could provide people with many goods essential for their material well-being and at the same time create a culture of solidarity. Since the informal economy is embedded in social relations, Polanyi believed that developing it would help in shaping the future orientation of the formal economy too.

Affinity with Catholic Social Teaching

At this point I wish to offer a few remarks on a topic that deserves a longer treatment, namely the affinity between Polanyi's social theory and the tradition of Catholic social teaching. The latter has been a topic of special interest to me over the years. In North America, Catholic social teaching attracted public attention through the pastoral letter on economic justice published by the American bishops in 1986[8] and a series of pastoral statements on social justice made by the Canadian bishops during the 1970s and 1980s.[9] Catholic social teaching affirms the ethical foundation of the economy and argues that an economic crisis is essentially a moral crisis. While recognizing the plurality of cultures, Catholic social teaching repudiates a radical ethical relativism and instead defends a common human nature shared by all. It also rejects the idea that human history is internally oriented towards progress. Thus Catholic social teaching repudiates the economic necessity implicit in liberal capitalism and scientific Marxism and insists instead that the social and economic structures are ultimately grounded in people's free activities, which means that people remain ethically responsible for them and could, if they exercised their political will, actually transform them. Catholic social teaching believes in the usefulness of markets, but it opposes the self-regulating market system and warns against the growing pervasiveness of the competitive mentality. It supports the cooperative movement and indeed favours cooperation on every level of the economy. Workers, according to Catholic teaching, are the subjects, not the objects of production: they are entitled to participate in the decisions that affect the work process and the spending of the wealth they co-produce with the owners and management. Ultimately workers are to be the co-owners of the giant workbench at which they labour. Catholic social teaching recognizes the need for economic planning and approves of government intervention in the economy. Finally, it endorses the principle of "subsidiarity," which protects smaller communities, local and regional, from the interference of higher powers as long as the smaller communities are capable of taking care of their own needs. Subsidiarity is a principle of decentralization – and, as we have seen – the decentralization of the economy is an important theme in Polanyi's work.

A COUNTER-MOVEMENT IN THE PRESENT

The economic crisis of today's society recalls the situation of the 1920s and 1930s, when the self-regulating market system, freed from all control, failed to provide jobs and bread for working people and caused social and cultural disintegration in their midst. During the decades after the Second World War, conditions changed for the better. Governments assumed greater responsibility for the well-being of their people. Pushed by the labour movement and social-democratic parties and guided by Keynesian economic principles, governments played an active role in revitalizing national economies and redistributing, through various social welfare measures, some of the wealth produced. The new state of affairs was marked by an unwritten contract between capitalist society and the working class guaranteeing full employment, social welfare, and respect for labour unions.

Then, for reasons that are still debated among economists, the historical situation changed and this contract was betrayed as governments introduced monetarist policies, encouraged the return to the self-regulating market, and promoted the globalization of the competitive economy. That is where we were are today. Since governments must now obey the laws of global competition and offer favourable conditions to industrial corporations to persuade them to remain in the country, they are no longer capable of protecting the economic interests of their people. We witness the massive increase of unemployment, the presence of hunger and homelessness, the decline of neighbourhoods, the break-up of communities, the spread of despair, and a growing sense of powerlessness. Polanyi has made us especially sensitive to the cultural and human consequences of the economic decline. What is taking place in many regions and urban neighbourhoods is social disintegration, which leaves people in a state of psychic pain.

Polanyi would have regarded the present globalization of the economy as completely insane. Having become dependent upon foods and clothing cheaply produced in far-away places, many regions and countries in the North suffer social and economic disintegration and lose the skills and the will to feed and clothe themselves. They are no longer able to sustain themselves physically and culturally by their own work. At the same time, regions and countries of the South that are obliged to produce goods for export to the North find themselves unable to feed, clothe, and house their own people. The globalization of the economy leads to a universal disembedding of the economy, even in areas such as farming, which until now have resisted economic rationalization and remained a way of life for family and community.

The return to the self-regulating market is accompanied by an intellectual current, reflected in the leading newspapers and other mass media, that praises contemporary capitalism as the high-point of human evolution. After the collapse of communism, the decline of Marxism, and the decimation of the democratic Left, the omnipresent message we receive is that an alternative to the present system is simply impossible. This dominant ideology, supported by post-modern indifference and shoulder-shrugging, prevents critical thinking from getting a hearing and undermines the cultural resources of social solidarity.

Are there any counter-movements in today's society? In the 1960s and 1970s we witnessed the emergence of many social movements, especially the civil rights movement, the women's movement, the peace movement, and the ecological movement. Sociologists such as Alain Touraine[10] and Claus Offe[11] interpreted these citizens' movements as forms of protest against the social and political conditions of those years, against the structures of social inequality, the nuclear arms race, and the damage done to the environment. Touraine suggested that what was happening was the self-organization of "civil society" in resistance to the bureaucratic power exercised both by the state and by large private corporations. In that period, many activists and some political thinkers were convinced that social movements were agents of radical reform which would succeed in transforming and humanizing modern society.

Some observers argue that social movements have lost momentum in recent years. The return to *laissez-faire* economics has produced new forms of dislocation and disintegration, prompting cultural pessimism and social passivity. Other observers prefer to point to the new orientation of social movements, even if they are reduced in size. In Canada – to give one example – social movements have supported the formation of the Action Canada Network, the nation-wide popular association that opposes the free trade agreements with the United States and Mexico. Threatened by a global economy that serves the interests of an élite, social movements have recognized that their own economic interests demand cooperative action, even if they should be in disagreement on some issues. The power of this alliance is hard to calculate. Though the Action Canada Network was unable to stop and, later, undo the free trade agreements, it affected and continues to affect a wide sector of the population.

One Canadian scholar has argued that in Polanyi's time there did exist a double movement and that he correctedly grasped its orientation, but that in our own time no such double movement is in sight.[12] In their introduction to a collection of essays entitled *The Legacy of Karl Polanyi,* Marguerite Mendell and Daniel Salée refute this pessimistic diagnosis. They elucidate the parallels between the economic situations of the 1920s and the 1990s and argue that several new currents in society correspond to Polanyi's theory of the double movement.[13] In my view, they are right. Polanyi still helps us to interpret the contemporary situation. There do exist counter-currents that seek to create social identity and protect habitation.

The first of these currents is evident on the right. We witness a disturbing cultural emphasis, often in extreme forms, on people's collective identities, whether this be in the emergence of excessive nationalism or regionalism, in new manifestations of religious orthodoxies, or in the defence of exclusively ethnic solidarities. Liberals and Marxists are puzzled by this development. Liberals expected people to choose the enhancement of their individual material benefits, and Marxists expected them to act according to the economic interest of their class. Yet Polanyi warned that, threatened by cultural breakdown and social disintegration, people often reaffirm or redefine their collective identities with a passion that submerges their own personal freedom and denies the human dignity of dissidents and outsiders.

During the 1930s the fascist movement in many countries was supported by the capitalist élite because it looked upon fascism as a bulwark against the communist threat. This is one reason why fascism became so successful. In my opinion, the present situation is quite different. Since communism has collapsed, the capitalist class has no interest in right-wing extremism and actually views it as a threat to the good order necessary for the flowering of the world economy. Dreadful as these right-wing radicals are, therefore they do not pose a serious threat to the Western democracies. Society must still offer vigorous opposition to the extreme right, but, if Polanyi's analysis is correct, this opposition must not be confined to police or security intervention but should include a collective effort to integrate these dislocated people into the social and economic institutions of their country.

There exists a second social current in present-day society that is a candidate for Polanyi's counter-movement. No longer believing that the government is capable of turning the economy around, some people in our society look for new forms of economic cooperation at the community level as well as in the industrial sector. Initiatives by local people in low-income neighboorhoods, combined with efforts of community organizations and often supported by financial help from business and government, have produced micro-systems of production that deal with local needs, such as common kitchens, jointly run stores, ventures to repair homes, and efforts to grow food in backyards. These initiatives include loan associations, set up by community organizations, which give local people access to capital at low interest rates that they can use for economic projects that serve the community. Similarly, both in the United States and Canada, committees have been set up in outlying regions to encourage local people to cooperate in the creation of autonomous economic development. And in one Canadian province in particular, Quebec, a long-standing tradition of cooperatism and social solidarity – generated by a French-speaking people living on a predominantly English-speaking continent – has produced a vital brand of alternative, community-based economics.[14] The development of these many and varied cooperative efforts constitutes a trend in society that Polanyi would recognize as a counter-movement.

Although this movement is not a vast undertaking visible to the uninitiated public, it is substantial and has been the object of social-scientific research. Accounts of its role in the United States include Harry Boyte's *The Backyard Revolution* (1981) and, more recently, Severyn Bruins and James Meehen's *Beyond the Market and the State: New Directions in Community Development* (1987). An analysis of its importance in Canada is found in David Ross and Peter Usher's *From the Roots Up: Economic Development As If Community Mattered* (1986). The movement's significance has been recognized by publicly instituted research agencies such as the Economic Council of Canada.[15]

The aims of the projects associated with this movement are not simply economic; on the contrary, their main purpose is social in nature. Through them, people learn to engage in conversation and planning, become partners in the same enterprise, develop friendships, and find meaning and even excitement in their lives. In the movement as a whole, people are rescued from their isolation, their helplessness, and their anomie. The result is the "re-embedding of economic activity in social relations." One scholar, recalling Polanyi's analysis of the substantive economy, has suggested that the popular movement of the late-twentieth century signifies "the return of reciprocity" in modern society.[16]

At a colloquium held in Montreal in 1988 dealing with the alternative economy, social scientists from western Europe and North America did not agree on the viability of the movement.[17] Some even described it as the self-exploitation of the poor. A few of them argued, first, that the people involved in the movement are unable to support it economically, and, second, that government and local business are willing put some money into this movement so that the people at the margin become involved and occupied – and thus unable to cause trouble. These critics also noted that even with help from outside, organizers of the movement tend to become exhausted and after a few years suffer "burn-out."

Yet the greater part of the assembled social scientists took a more positive view. Their research convinced them of the viability of these experiments in social and economic renewal. Enthusiastic support for the popular movement was expressed by members of the colloquium who were not only observers but also active participants in various collective efforts to promote alternative models of economic development. They argued that the movement not only served the social integration of marginalized people but also represented an experiment in economic democracy that may well teach the whole of society a lesson for the future.

Cooperative efforts at the community level are matched by similar projects in the business sector. In the past, workers contributed to industrial production only through their muscles: they were not allowed to contribute with their intelligence. It is argued today that production can be greatly improved if managers allow workers to become participants at all levels of the industrial process. It is also argued that the class conflict between capital and labour carried on within the industry damages production and hurts the owners as well as the workers. Can conflict in industry be replaced by cooperation? There are today specific enterprises where both managers and workers, aware of the self-destructive potential of perpetual conflict, have sought an industrial system based on cooperation. This effort, sometimes called neo-corporatism, is hotly debated in the labour movement.[18] Is industrial cooperation a ploy used by management to pacify workers without granting them the power to improve their conditions? Or does management offer workers sufficient power to make them true partners and thus capable of looking after their own interests? There are growing numbers of industries where managers and workers have found ways to improve the level of cooperation between them.

In Quebec the two trends, the movement at the community level and the new industrial cooperation, are quite strong. They are referred to by the French word *concertation.* We also hear the expression *Québec Inc.*, which, while referring mainly to the growing involvement of the state in business life, suggest that economically Quebec is becoming a more cooperative society.[19] The term *concertation* can easily be used by politicians and owners of industry as an empty promise that disguises the real situation. This sort of *concertation* could also tempt labour unions to seek improved conditions for their own members while forgetting about solidarity with the unemployed and the marginalized. Still, it would be cynical to suppose that there are no conditions under which *concertation* in industrial production would significantly improve economic performance and at the same time make work into a cooperative activity.

As critical people lose hope of changing society through the vehicle of social-democratic political parties, they come to believe that what demands practical support are cooperative efforts both in building a community-based, alternative economy and in institutionalizing *concertation* in more democratically operated industries. This shift has been recognized in the Christian churches, especially in Quebec. The Catholic Church, which represents a minority in modern Quebec, has expressed support for the popular movement in pastoral letters. Among several such letters, the Labour Day Statement of 1 May 1992 on democratizing the economy,[20] which strongly favoured the creation of more cooperative economic institutions at all levels, is especially important. The statement recommends the introduction of more democratic procedures in industrial and commercial companies as well as the multiplication of small-scale cooperative ventures among the people deserted and damaged by the market system. Such joint efforts, the bishops hold, not only satisfy the economic needs of people in neglected areas but also generate social solidarity and thus change the quality of life in the community.

The Catholic monthly review *Relations* – of whose editorial board I am a member – decided several years ago to offer intellectual support to the popular movement, encourage the participants, make known its achievements in the cities and the outlying regions of the province, and use both utilitarian and ethical arguments to urge the public and the government to continue and, if possible, increase their assistance to the local, community-based economy.[21]

On the practical level, bishops in the outer regions of Quebec – accompanied by Catholic social-justice groups – cooperate with various citizens' groups in creating local enterprises that are designed to alleviate their economic problems and integrate and give new life to their communities.[22] Using Karl Polanyi's terms, we can say that the bishops advocate the return of institutionalized reciprocity and the "re-embedding" of people's economic activities in the social relations that constitute their community.

The network of Catholic social-justice groups and the body of the Quebec bishops also support the movement Solidarité Populaire Québec, which brings together people neglected by the market system and seeks to articulate with their help a vision of a more just and participatory Quebec. After this movement succeeded in attracting the cooperation of organized labour unions, it convened in March 1994 a large *forum de la solidarité*, which was attended by a thousand activists representing unions and a wide spectrum of popular groups and networks, including Catholic organizations and the Quebec bishops. The aim of this event was to give new strength to a movement that struggles against the government's neo-liberal economic policies and promotes cooperation and participation at all levels of society.

What I conclude from this cursory glance at Quebec society is that the movement to create alternative, local, or regional models of economic development is a candidate for the counter-movement described in Polanyi's social theory. Equivalent movements are found in all capitalist countries, even if they are still small and threatened by exhaustion or lack of support. Though these alternative ventures are unable to challenge global corporate capitalism, they create solidarity, make life saner and happier for many people, and produce new ideas and practices that may eventually help to transform the present economic system. The great attraction of Polanyi's social theory is that it offers hope, fosters action, and recognizes the hidden potentialities of ordinary people.

4
Ethics in a Pluralistic Society

I now wish to deal in a new way with the question as to whether Polanyi's theory of the double movement is credible. In the previous chapter I argued, with the support of a good number of political economists, that even in the present neo-liberal decade such a counter-movement does exist. People continue to defend their habitation against the inroads of the self-regulating market system. Yet the movement is small. Since it exists at the community level, will it ever be strong enough to affect the dominant structures?

If Polanyi were a functionalist, he would argue that by its own inner dynamism every society, shaken by unexpected and destabilizing interventions, produces a corrective response and moves ineluctably towards a new equilibrium. In functionalist theory, society is a complex social and cultural system that affects people's minds and prompts them to act in a certain way, without their necessarily being aware that what they are doing contributes to the restoration of society's equilibrium. According to this reasoning, society acts, as it were, behind people's backs. Yet Polanyi was not a functionalist. When he claimed that society has a tendency to protect itself, he supported his case by listing the concrete movements that seek to correct and overcome the distorting impact of the self-regulating market. His proposal, therefore, is only as good as the empirical arguments that can be mustered in its favour.

Polanyi holds that, because humans are social and in fact ethical beings, they are likely to protect their community and the land on which they live. In the previous chapter I showed that a small counter-movement does exist in the present. At this point I wish to ask whether there are ethical resources in contemporary society that enable people to transcend the dominant individualism and choose more communitarian values. When I speak of ethical resources, I am thinking not only of ideas. The ethos of a society is produced not so much by ideas as by the institutions in which people live and the symbols mediated by their culture.

In the following discussion, then, I summarize Karl Polanyi's ethical viewpoint, contrast it with the dominant ethos of capitalist society, and inquire whether the cultural symbols and social institutions of present-day society still provide resources for an ethic of community and social solidarity. This argument is intended to strengthen the realism of Polanyi's theory.

POLANYI'S ETHICS

According to Karl Polanyi, ethics play an indispensable part in the constitution of society. He believed, as we saw in the second chapter, that humans are essentially ethical beings. Though he does not offer a consistent ethical theory, he does suppose that people, wherever they may be, hear a summons to love their neighbour and assume responsibility for their community. Sometimes Polanyi suggests that this ethical summons is derived from the great world religions and secular wisdom and is mediated by culture. At other times he suggests that the ethical summons is an essential part of people's basic self-recognition: mature persons experience themselves as responsible for their *Lebensweg*, their daily lives in the company of others. An in-depth look at the basic experience of being human, Polanyi proposes, reveals the human being's ethical vocation. Sometimes Polanyi uses metaphysical language to suggest that the ethical vocation is part of human nature itself. Just as we are by nature rational beings endowed with freedom, so too we are ethical beings endowed with responsibility. In other passages Polanyi appeals to a metaphysics derived from biblical revelation, according to which society itself has a God-given nature. When this nature is violated by unjust social and economic structures, it summons people to struggle for the transformation of their society.

Polanyi holds that, as historical conditions change, love and responsibility also assume new meaning. As societies become more complex and its members increasingly interdependent, the love of neighbour is expanded and transformed into social solidarity. And as global society itself becomes increasingly interdependent, every human being becomes our neighbour and love begins to generate universal social solidarity. To repeat a sentence I have used in my own writings, the love of neighbour in societies marked by grave injustice transforms itself into solidarity with the victims and the impulse to act so that the heavy burden of suffering may be lifted from their shoulders. This view is, I think, in keeping with Polanyi's concept of ethical developmnent.

The understanding of responsibility has expanded in similar fashion. Polanyi argues, we recall, that the Enlightenment brought forth a new sense of personal responsiblity, a new maturity, urging people to question traditional institutions and inherited ethical norms and to decide for themselves on rational grounds what is the good and how they should act. When Polanyi mentions the Enlightenment in this context, what he has in mind is not John Locke's utilitarian ethics, defined by man's rational material self-interest, but rather the ethics of responsibility for the whole that is found in Kant and Hegel and the humanistic tradition generated by the Enlightenment. Yet what responsibility for the whole means changes as human power to transform society increases. As modern means of communication and transportation transform the globe into a single sphere of influence, individuals and their societies are held to assume ethical responsibility for the entire human family.

Polanyi also demonstrates special respect for nature, especially for the land on which we live. He criticizes the instrumental concept of nature that characterizes industrial society. He laments modern, urban man's estrangement from nature and suggests that people's familiarity with nature, at least through gardening – which he himself practised – would have a beneficial impact on their world view. In addition, Polanyi was convinced that under present conditions solidarity and responsibility reach beyond the human family currently living on this earth to include the populations of the future. Because he saw ethics as grounded in metaphysics, he believed that we are obliged to protect the resources of the earth for subsequent generations.

The idea that ethics plays such an important role in people's lives is central to Polanyi's social and economic theory. For him, the emergence of social movements determined to set limits to the self-regulating market is rooted in the ethical resources of ordinary people ready to defend their community, their habitation, and even their society as whole. People are by nature ethical and creative. They have the inner capacity to invent new forms of social and economic arrangements which protect the values that define their communities. Polanyi held that a social movement bent on transforming society would improve the conditions of life only if its participants were guided by an ethical vision. The struggle to overcome injustice must be inspired by more than legitimate self-interest: it also calls for solidarity, sacrifice, and self-transcendence.

Polanyi, we recall, used humanity's ethical vocation to offer an argument for what he called "the new socialism." It is impossible, he argued, to live a responsible ethical life in an economic system that operates according to impersonal laws and prevents the actors from knowing the impact of their actions on other people. The coffee and sugar we buy and use every day, to mention a simple example, have effects upon the lives of the people who produce them, effects of which we are often ignorant but which we have to understand if our actions are to be responsible. Ethics calls for a transparent economic system where we can estimate the impact of producing, buying, and selling upon society.

THE DOMINANT UTILITARIANISM

Polanyi's ethical reflections are at odds with the dominant ethos of present-day society, which is utilitarianism. It defines the *bonum* as utility or rational material self-interest. In essence, it is an ethos mediated by the market system, since the market is a mechanism of exchange demanding that each player seek to get the best deal. By generating competition, so the reasoning goes, the market system urges people to work harder and at the same time tames their greed. Adam Smith believed that the market was a marvellous invention that transformed people's self-interested activity into socially useful labour serving the common good.

Utilitarianism is rooted in the British philosophical tradition. In the seventeenth century John Locke defined human beings in terms of their *conatus*, meaning their struggle for self-preservation. Though he was not the first, Locke broke with the classical tradition and subsequent Christian teaching, both of which had defined human beings through their orientation towards the true and the good. By contrast, Locke thought that human beings were engaged in a never-ending conflict and competition in which all were afraid that their neighbours might steal their property or even take their lives. People, indeed, lived in constant fear. In order to transcend their fear and pursue their material well-being in an enlightened, rational way, human beings entered into a social contract, conceded a portion of their power to a government they set up, and assigned to this government the task of protecting their life and property and the freedoms they needed to pursue their interests. Rational material self-interest, then, grounds the liberal state, just as it defines the capitalist system. In liberal society people no longer live in fear. They may not love their neighbours nor be loved by them, but they are no longer afraid of them since their civil rights are protected by government.

Charles Taylor has made the point that utilitarian self-interest does not account for the ethical passion with which John Locke and like-minded philosophers sought to reform society.[1] Locke passionately defended tolerance and pluralism against the absolute claims made by the Tudor monarchy, an intellectual activity for which he suffered persecution and went several times into exile. The utilitarian philosophers of the nineteenth century, such as Jeremy Bentham and John Stuart Mill, were also deeply involved in reforming their society and thereby transcended their own philosophical theory. Mill even tried to find utilitarian arguments for self-sacrifice and social solidarity: he attempted to demonstrate that it is advantageous for people in the long run to support the greatest good for the greatest number. Yet Mill's arguments were weak. If one begins with a concept of man as defined by the *conatus* and of the good defined as the "useful," it is impossible to arrive at an ethic of universal solidarity and personal self-transcendence.[2]

Still, from the end of the nineteenth century on, progressive liberals in Britain offered utilitarian arguments for the welfare state. They argued, for instance, that an excessive gap between rich and poor destabilized society and disturbed the social peace, which was needed for the advancement of industry and commerce, and that it was therefore imperative to achieve a certain redistribution of wealth. They also argued that, since industrial technology had greatly increased the production of goods, workers should be paid higher wages so that they too can become customers and thus support the economy. In liberal society governments must legitimize the welfare legislation they introduce with utilitarian arguments demonstrating that the new laws serve the material well-being of society as a whole and hence indirectly also the interests of the middle class.

TOWARD A NEW ETHICS

Polanyi upheld an ethics of social solidarity, respect for nature, and personal responsibility transcending utilitarianism. Yet Polanyi was not a Kantian inasmuch as he did not regard material self-interest as unethical. Following classical philosophy and the Catholic tradition, he thought that there was nothing wrong with self-interested activity. People have every right to struggle for improvement in the material conditions of their lives. Utility is ethically problematic and culturally dangerous only when it is the sole motivating force in people's lives. Polanyi agreed with Max Weber that people tend to act from a variety of motives and that collective social action is most effective when the motives of the actors include material self-interest, ethical vision, and strong feeling.

It is not without interest that Catholic theology looks upon self-interest or self-love as ethically acceptable since the self is created, accepted, and loved by God. What is sinful, in this theology, is exaggerated self-love, for self-centredness violates the demands of other-love and the norms of justice. To clarify the concept of self-love or self-realization, some Catholic and humanistic philosophers distinguish between "utilitarian self-interest" and "eudaemonistic self-interest," the latter referring to the universal human quest for happiness and fulfilment. This quest, they argue, actually leads to self-transcendence and gratuitous love because human beings find their happiness and self-realization precisely in forgetting themselves, turning towards another in love, and surrendering themselves to a transcendent value, even to God. Polanyi would have found this philosophy congenial. He too believed that people were led by an ethical summons to an ever wider sense of solidarity and responsibility, and that in resisting this call people become superficial, restless, and unfaithful to the best in themselves.

Confronted as we are by the enormous problems of ecological disaster, world hunger, massive unemployment, and seemingly unappeasable armed conflicts, many concerned thinkers propose that we are in need of a new ethics of solidarity, responsibility, and respect for nature.[3] For Polanyi, this new ethics is actually the old ethics responding to the new conditions of the present. Yet in a society dominated by capitalist culture and characterized by individualism, utilitarianism, and relativism, where do we find the spiritual recourses for a new ethics?

The authors who propose the new ethics usually do not reply to this question. Yet ethics is more than a set of good ideas; ethics also communicates a sense of obligation. Ethics is grounded in the imperative, not the indicative. Polanyi believed that the spiritual resources for an ethics of solidarity are available in people's daily lives through the cultural impact of religious tradition and also through the call of their conscience, which is a dimension of human existence itself.

Is Polanyi excessively hopeful? Is it reasonable to expect the emergence of a new ethics in today's pluralistic market-societies? In this chapter I name several cultural and institutional forces in contemporary society that do promote an ethos beyond utilitarian individualism. Whether they will be strong enough to resist the dominant trend, I do not know. But human resources are available that can inspire people to move beyond the logic of the market and display solidarity, responsibility, and respect of nature. I see especially three factors that deserve attention: cultural resources for a more communal ethics; collective experiences that generate new ethical responses; and political and social institutions that give rise to social solidarity.

CULTURAL RESOURCES

Polanyi had great confidence in the world religions. Though these traditions are highly ambiguous, fostering cooperation as well as hostility, they do contain values that offer support for solidarity, responsibility, and respect for nature. This is demonstrated, for instance, by the joint declarations of the World Conference on Religion and Peace, an organization created in the 1970s.[4] In these declarations the representatives of the world religions recognize that their traditions have often fostered injustice and violence in human history, but that on a deeper level they are also bearers of the ideals of justice and peace which are destined to reconcile the human family. That the latter ideals acquire a new centrality in the practice of the world religions is the aim and purpose of the World Conference on Religion and Peace.

The turn of the Christian churches to solidarity, responsibility, and respect for nature is documented at the Geneva-based World Council of Churches and in the more recent social teaching of the Catholic Church. In each of the churches there exist significant movements that support and promote the new ethics.

There are also secular humanistic traditions that communicate values beyong utility and produce generous reactions to contemporary problems. Some humanists still retain the classical notion that humans are by nature oriented towards the true, the good, and the beautiful. They are deeply troubled by John Locke's liberal and capitalist concept of the human as defined by the *conatus.* Some of these humanists see themselves as heirs of Plato: well-known names among this group are Simone Weil and George Grant. Others locate themselves in the Aristotelian tradition: this is true especially but not exclusively of Catholic social philosophers. Alasdair MacIntyre also stands in that tradition. Some thinkers, especially the Frankfurt School of Critical Theory, attach great importance to Kant's understanding of practical reason, according to which people validly postulate as true those principles of reality without which their collective existence could not be truly human. For Kant, practical reason offers an entry into metaphysics, affirming, for instance, the existence of the soul. For some contemporary thinkers, practical reason opens the door to a substantive ethics. Intellectual heirs of Hegel and the Romantic philosophers also hold that people constitute a single human family, are responsible for one another, and hear the call to universal solidarity. In his celebrated *Sources of the Self,* Charles Taylor rereads the modern philosophers to show that the ethics brought forth by the Enlightenment greatly transcends the utilitarian perspective associated with the capitalist market and a certain kind of empiricism.

Whereas religious traditions are sustained by ordinary people and embodied in their lives, philosophers influence only an élite. Still, philosophical ideas have cultural power if they confirm people's lived experiences. Some social scientists – especially those influenced by Emile Durkheim – claim that despite the dominant utilitarianism people continue to relate to another on the most basic level through trust, gratitude, and friendship.[5] They argue, with Polanyi, that without virtue in people's personal lives society could not be sustained for long. If this analysis is correct, then the philosophical traditions mentioned above exert cultural influence because they support people in their exercise of love and generosity.

The cultural resources for an ethics of solidarity also incude the symbols and stories that dwell in a culture and affect people's ethical vision. On the whole, sociologists recognize more clearly than political scientists that each society celebrates a myth of its origin and that people are more deeply attached than they realize to the images of their collective identity. Regional, national, and continental collectivities are often bearers of rites and symbols that communicate a social vision and a communal ethics. What tradition allows an American president to plead with his people not to ask, "What can my country do for me?" but rather to transcend the ethics of utility and ask, "What can I do for my country?" The authority behind this appeal is surely derived from the American nation's myth of origin, from what Robert Bellah has called America's "civil religion,"[6] which includes the call to solidarity and collective responsibility.

No one knows how strong these symbols and stories are in a society that is now marked by economic decline. Yet one must not exclude the possibility that in times of great distress these myths acquire a new effectiveness and enable people to make sacrifices for the common good.

NEW COLLECTIVE EXPERIENCES

Another source of the new ethic are the creative, collective responses to new historical developments. One startling example of this is the Universal Declaration of Human Rights, promulgated by the United Nations in 1948. The declaration offers no religious or philosophical arguments for the high dignity of individual persons and their communities, upon which human rights are based. Metaphysical arguments would only have divided the national communities. What the declaration proclaims is that, after the devastation and crimes against humanity that marked the Second World War, the nations of the world pledge themselves to uphold the personal and collective rights of all human beings. Here the response to outrage is a new ethical stance.

The reaction to massive evil is not necessarily outrage and a new sense of solidarity. Some people respond to historical disaster by becoming fragmented, depressed, or even cynical, desperately attached to their own survival or even willing to support an authoritarian regime. Still, theologians have attached importance to people's creative reactions to massive evil. Thus Edward Schillebeeckx has argued that there exist among vast numbers of people profound experiences of an ethical nature that consist of revulsion from evil and the impulse to help.[7] The passionate revulsion from actions that cause human suffering is joined by the strong conviction that such actions can and must be stopped. At certain moments of history, these so-called "contrast experiences" have raised humanity's threshold of moral awareness.

An often-cited example is the abolition of slavery. At one time slavery was recognized in Western history as ethically acceptable: classical Greek philosophy defended it and even the Bible did not repudiate it unambiguously. Though church authorities occasionally expressed their disapproval of slavery, it was only in the eighteenth century that certain secular and religious humanists were so outraged by the institution of slavery that they started a social movement that would eventually lead to its abolition. In this instance, "contrast experiences" shared by many produced a new ethic that, joined by political struggles and favoured by changing economic conditions, was destined to transform the moral awareness of Western society.

What is the foundation of such contrast experiences? On this point, philosophers differ. Is there a moral sense woven into human nature itself that reaches our consciousness through important historical experiences? Are these experiences cultural consequences of the Enlightenment, the age of critical reason? Has humanity a hidden divine orientation that reveals its deepest meaning only in historical struggles for the good life? Does the warmth, love, and ecstasy experienced by babies in their mothers' arms lay the psychological foundation for the quest of a global society based on universal solidarity? Since this chapter is concerned with ethics in modern, pluralistic society, the theoretical answer people give to such questions is not important. What counts is the existence of these contrast experiences as ethical resources in contemporary society.

Moral outrage is a response to great evil, past, present, or approaching. The human response to the threat of future evil is at times also capable of creating a sense of sacrifice and solidarity. An example is the experience of the people of England during the Second World War. When threatened by the superior force of the enemy, English people were gripped by an uncommon spirit of sacrifice and solidarity which transcended even the clearly drawn class divisions of their society. Similarly, an approaching environmental disaster may summon forth an ethical commitment on the part of society to create an alternative culture of simplicity and self-limitation.

Besides moral outrage and response to catastrophe, there seems to exist a universal impulse to support the weak, an impulse that in a new situation may generate a new ethics. Confucian philosophers think that people are spontaneously generous.[8] They argue that someone seeing a child drowning in a lake instinctively reaches out to rescue the little person. Research done on the motives of men and women who hid Jews fleeing Nazi persecution has revealed that in most instances these courageous people could not articulate the reasons for their action. Their response, they said, was spontaneous: there was no other choice, they simply followed their impulse.

Paul Ricoeur has offered a brilliant analysis of the imperative experienced by people to assume responsibility for "the fragile,"[9] by whom he means persons threatened by natural weakness or endangered by violence. People recognize this imperative, he argues, through a certain feeling affecting them on a fundamental level. We feel ourselves enjoined by the fragile to care, to offer help, and, more important, to foster growth and sustain fulfilment. In the presence of the weak and the threatened we are addressed by a summons to take care of them and assume responsibility for them, even if we are unable or unwilling to do so. This ethical imperative accounts for the ordinary experience of people as they spontaneously reach out to hold the person who stumbles at their side, and it explains the extraordinary experience of people who decide upon an impulse to rescue others in moments of great danger, even if they risk their own security in doing so.

For Paul Ricoeur, our instinctive compassion for the fragile reveals that human beings are inter-independent, not isolated, individuals. We are open to each other and, in heeding the call of our fellow human beings for care and love, we realize our own potential and become more truly faithful to ourselves.

In the present historical situation, Paul Ricoeur proposes, responsibility for the fragile has a new and special meaning. What has become fragile is humanity itself, rendered insecure and profoundly threatened by major calamities, especially the ongoing deterioration of the environment and the creation of a single world economy that pushes ever greater sectors of humanity into misery and death. To assume responsibility for the natural environment and create an economic framework that allows all people to thrive will demand not only inventiveness but also an ethical commitment on the part of society to selflessness and self-limitation. This new ethics, Ricoeur argues, is within our reach because of our natural impulse to care for the fragile.

INSTITUTIONAL FACTORS

So far we have looked at cultural resources and new social responses capable of promoting the new ethics – the old ethics from Polanyi's point of view. Yet, since people's self-understanding and moral vision are to a large extent created by the institutions to which they belong and in which they participate, I wish to examine whether there are institutions in modern society that generate an ethic that transcends utilitarianism.

The primary institution to which we belong and which affects our mental outlook is the market. In its simplest form the market is a game where each person tries to advance his or her own material advantage. When the market became the dominant institution in society, people grew increasingly individualistic and began to view their neighbours as rivals and competitors. The classical economists believed that the market revealed the very nature of human beings, that people were utility maximizers – rational calculators of their material benefit. Because people's economic behaviour was predictable, these economists regarded economics as a science in the strict sense.

Recently some economists have argued that the complex modern market actually prompts people to make choices of a different kind. These economists call their discipline "social ecomomics." Charles Wilber, professor of social economics at Notre Dame University in the United States, has argued that under conditions of interdependence and imperfect information, rational self-interest frequently leads to economically irrational results.[10] In the past, economists supposed that each player was independent and had perfect information about the conditions of the game. But in the complex market of industrial society, the success of economic ventures depends on the cooperation of many players and hence is endangered by purely self-interested choices. Choices defined by material self-interest alone undermine the willingess of the other players to cooperate. More than that, since their willingness to cooporate can never be predicted scientifically, economic ventures are entered upon with imperfect information and undemonstrable assumptions. The assumptions one makes about the behaviour of other people influence how they will actually behave so that self-interested choices, assuming that the others are also maximizers of their own advantage, actually create conditions of conflict rather than cooperation. Therefore, economic undertakings demand "strategic," not self-interested, action.

Particularly in periods of economic decline, people have a common interest in improving their material position. But if each group of economic actors – employers and their employees – focuses on what wil bring it the greatest advantage, they will create a conflict situation and neither will reach the common goal they desire. Thus, Adam Smith's "invisible hand" not only fails to serve the common good but in fact undermines it. Today's complex market calls for strategic choices, choices based on the awareness of interdependence and the indeterminate nature of the response of others. Strategic actions take into consideration the advantage of others. Through strategic actions persons support the goals of others for the sake of realizing their own proper ends. At the same time, strategic actions as here defined involve more than a redefinition of rational self-interest because they rest on the assumption that other people are cooperators. There is an element of hope in strategic economic decisions and hence a moral hazard, an openness to failure, which demands a spririt of generosity to create and sustain a climate of cooperation.

These theoretical reflections are confirmed by the emergence of the new corporatism in many European countries, supported by labour unions, management, and social-democratic governments. In chapter 3 we saw that neo-corporatist experiments are being tried in Quebec and Canada. Though the Lockean theory that humans are by nature competitors, each bent on his or her own material advantage, is still accepted by many social and economic theorists and above all by the decision makers in society, our complex market actually calls for and in many instances produces economic behaviour that reflects a more cooperative understanding of humankind.

Also present in society are democratic institutions. They too affect people's values, dreams, and aspirations. John Locke grounded democratic theory purely and simply in the rational self-interest of individual citizens. By way of contrast, I wish to argue that democracy, whatever its theoretical foundation, is an institution that creates a desire among people to participate in the making of the decisions that affect their lives. The democratic process, involving public debate, freedom of speech, civil liberties, representative government, and transparent procedures of governmental decision making, has given rise to a yearning among people to become responsible agents of their society. While the early forms of Western democracy confined the vote and responsible citizenship to the property-owning burghers, the democratic process created popular aspirations and historical forces that sought to extend democratic rights to the excluded: the propertyless, the workers, and, eventually, women. The democratic revolution could not be stopped. Democracy became stable, at least for a while, only when participation was offered to all citizens.

Because in contemporary culture people desire to be responsible subjects of their social world, they are frustrated when their democratic governments act undemocratically. In fact, people increasingly believe that the present form of democracy does not provide them with sufficient opportunity to influence the making of public policy. In contemporary society, people feel uncomfortable in any institutions that exclude them from sharing in the decisions that affect their lives. That is why the American sociologist C. Wright Mills argued that there is a contradiction between democracy and capitalism. The capitalist organizations he knew were hierarchically structured and excluded, on principle, workers and employees from the policy-making process. That is also the reason why Catholics in democratic societies are restless within their own church, where they are excluded from participating in decisions that closely touch their personal lives.

Owing to the cultural impact of democracy, people believe that they are meant to be responsible agents of the institutions to which they belong. They desire such responsibility not simply because it will allow them to protect their own interests but also and especially because it is demanded by their own self-respect. The democratic process initiates people to a new self-perception, one that transcends the purely utilitarian perspective. The practice of democracy inspires a sense of the dignity of men and women, a dignity that entitles them to be the subjects of their social world. When institutions prevent people from acting as responsible subjects, they suffer grave injustice, are kept from their human destiny, and become victims of alienation. This radical conviction, articulated in the writings of the young Marx, has since been almost universally endorsed in democratic cultures. Among its defenders is Pope John Paul II.[11]

Whereas the feudal order with its inherited hierarchies ascribed different degrees of honour to the various estates in society, the democratic order created the belief that citizens have equal dignity. From the nineteenth century on, political struggles forced democratic governments to offer assistance to the poor and protect workers from the heavy burdens inflicted on them by their capitalist employers. Eventually there emerged in society an awareness that the dignity of men and women entitled them to the satisfaction of their basic needs, especially food, shelter, health care, and education. An ethical conviction began to spread in democratic societies that, in addition to civil rights, citizens also enjoy socio-economic rights. With the arrival of social democracy, a certain ethos of solidarity became almost universally acknowledged in western Europe and Canada and gradually in the United States.

We now come to doctors, nurses, teachers, engineers, judges, and so on – all of them organized in institutions with codes of behaviour assuring that these professionals serve the well-being of their clients and the good of society. Of course, while the professions are services to society, they are also sources of income and forms of business for those who practise them. There is a certain conflict in the professions between the altruistic ethos defined by their official codes and the material self-interest that tempts professionals to regard their work simply as a source of wealth and status in society. Yet to claim that professionals as a rule behave as self-promoters would be excessively cynical. Despite evidence for a certain decline of the professional ethos, I am prepared to argue that the professions still encourage an ethic of service among the greater part of their members and thus make an important contribution to the creation of the culture of solidarity.

Finally an ethic promoting the common good is also created by social movements: labour unions, cooperatives, women's organizations, regional development bodies, religious communities, citizens' associations, environmental forums, peace organizations, and so on. There exists in Canada an entire network of groups and communities critical of the established institutions. These groups and communities express and communicate an ethos that includes a utilitarian dimension but extends beyond it to strive for social solidarity. The new spirit is symbolized in the Action Canada Network, mentioned in chapter 3, a large, nation-wide cooperative association supported by labour unions, popular groups of various kinds, and church committees. The impact of social movements upon people's consciousness should not be underestimated. They generate an ethic of solidarity among a significant sector of society.

SUMMATION

This inquiry has dealt with the questions raised by Polanyi's social theory. Is there, as Polanyi and many other social thinkers held, an ethic of solidarity and responsibility implicit in history that summons people in times of crises to defend their community, their habitation, and the natural environment? Polanyi believed that such an ethic of solidarity, combined with people's desire to survive and live dignified lives, was the social source of what he called the double movement. He found historical evidence for such a counter-current in the successful effort, beginning in the second part of the nineteenth century, to impose limits on the self-regulating market system. And he demonstrated that, in the history of humanity prior to the arrival of industrial capitalism and the self-regulating market, people's economic activities were embedded in their society and thus served to strengthen their social bonds, their cultural matrix, and their collective identity. The rootedness of humanity in its history and the growing strength of the counter-current after the Great Depression convinced Polanyi that a great transformation would take place following the Second World War. This transformation would create a social-democratic consciousness in the Western world and begin to re-embed people's economic activities into their cultural and social existence.

Recent decades have shown that Polanyi was wrong. But the question remains whether the current globalization of the free market system will again be challenged by a counter-movement based on people's collective desire to protect their community, their land, and their habitation. What I have tried to show in this book is that Polanyi's theory of the double movement is not the result of wishful thinking. A counter-movement is evident in today's world. Found primarily in the disadvantaged sectors of society, this counter-movement mobilizes people to create alternative, small-scale models of economic development that help them to lighten their economic burden and at the same time produce a sense of community and social solidarity. Admittedly, the movement is small but it does exist and who is to say that it will not grow?

I have tried to show that, despite the individualism and utilitarianism that dominate contemporary society, our world is not bereft of traditional values, historical symbols, and social institutions that generate corrective cultural currents and bring forth an ethic of communal concern and social solidarity. Even if this is no scientific proof of Polanyi's proposal, it sustains its credibility.

Polanyi realized that a prediction about future developments can never be proven valid. For the reaction of people to such a prediction, whether they affirm or reject it, becomes itself an historical factor that influences future development. The hope produced by Polanyi's theory delivers people from a sense of powerlessness and strengthens the counter-movement in their society. It is precisely the absence of "necessity" in Polanyi's theory and his recognition of human agency that make his ideas persuasive and liberating. Polanyi believed that in pursuing his research and writing his books he made a practical contribution to the counter-movement that sought to rescue people from the social disintegration and economic ills produced by the self-regulating market system. In a modest way, the purpose of this book is the same.

Notes

PREFACE

1 Thomas Hueglin, "Have We Read the Wrong Authors: On the Relevance of Johannes Althusius," *Studies in Political Thought*, vol. 1 (1992) 75–93.

2 For an introduction to Polanyi's thought, see two collections of essays: Kari Polanyi-Levitt, ed., *The Life and Work of Karl Polanyi* (Montreal: Black Rose Books 1990); and Marguerite Mendell and Daniel Salée, eds., *The Legacy of Karl Polanyi* (New York: St Martin's Press 1991).

3 I wish to mention two papers: Christopher Lind, "How Karl Polanyi's Moral Economy Can Help Religious and Other Social Critics," given at the 3rd International Karl Polanyi Conference, Milan, 1990; and Jordan Bishops, "Karl Polanyi and Christian Socialism," given at the 4th International Karl Polanyi Conference, Montreal, 1992.

CHAPTER I

1 Karl Polanyi, *The Great Transformation* (Boston: Beacon Press, 1957), 73.

2 Ibid., 83.

3 The title of chapter 3 in *The Great Transformation* is "Habitation versus Improvement" (33). See also 249.

4 My article "L'origine de la crise écologique: la contribution de Karl Polanyi," in José Prades, ed., *Environnement et développement* (Montréal: Fides 1991), 147–63, contains much of the material of this first chapter. Yet in that article I still wondered whether Polanyi was a functionalist thinker.

5 *The Great Transformation*, 46.

6 Ibid., ch. 7, 77–85.

7 Ibid., 78.

8 Polanyi's analysis of the Speedhamland Settlement is more complex than set down in this abbreviated account.

9 *The Great Transformation*, 138.

10 Ibid., 146.

11 Ibid., 132.

12 Ibid., 178.

13 Ibid.

14 Ibid., 181.

15 Ibid., 184.

CHAPTER 2

1 See György Litvan, "Democratic and Socialist Values in Karl Polanyi's Thought," in Mendell and Selée, eds. *The Legacy of Karl Polanyi*, 251–71, 253.

2 Abraham Rotstein (and Gerald Berthoud), "The Seductive Market," a paper given at the 3rd International Karl Polanyi Conference, Milan, 1990.

3 These papers are available in the archives of the Karl Polanyi Institute of Montreal at Concordia University's School of Community and Public Administration.

4 "Polanyi sur Marx et le marxisme: Textes inédits de Karl Polanyi," présentation de Marguerite Mendell, *Interventions économiques*, no. 18 (fall 1987), 241–53.

5 Prior to the 1920s, theologians of social justice constituted a minority in the Protestant churches. In German-speaking lands, they included thinkers such as Christoph Blumhardt, Leonard Ragaz, and Karl Barth; in Great Britain, they were a small band of Anglican theologians involved in what they called Christian Socialism; and in the United States and Canada, theologians of the "social gospel" foreshadowed later social-justice theory. As for the Catholic Church, papal teaching on social justice, beginning with Pope Leo XIII's encyclical *Rerum novarum* in 1891, offered an ethical critique of liberal capitalism, but it lacked the egalitarian perspective found in Polanyi and the Protestant thinkers mentioned above. See John Cort, *Christian Socialism* (Maryknoll, N.Y.: Orbis Books 1988).

6 See Daniel Salée, "Explaining Social Change," a paper given at the 3rd International Karl Polanyi Conference, which shows that Polanyi transcended the agency-structure dilemma. A corrective emphasis on agency is returning in contemporary sociology. See Anthony Giddens, *Central Problems in Social Theory* (Berkeley, Calif: University of California Press 1983), and Alain Touraine, *Return of the Actor: Social Theory in Post-industrial Society* (Minneapolis, Minn.: University of Minnesota Press 1988).

7 Abraham Rotstein, "The Reality of Society: Karl Polanyi's Philosophical Perspective," in Polanyi-Levitt, ed. *The Life and Work of Karl Polanyi*, 98–109, 109.

8 Karl Polanyi, "The Essence of Fascism," in John Lewis, Karl Polanyi, and Donald D. Kitchin, eds., *Christianity and the Social Revolution* (New York: Charles Scribner's 1936), 359–96. The German version is published in Karl Polanyi, *Oekonomie und Gesellschaft* (Frankfurt: Suhrkamp 1979), 91–128.

9 *The Great Transformation*, 127–8.

10 For an introductory essay to Macmurray's work, see Jack Costello, "John Macmurray: Freedom in Community," *The Ecumenist* (second series), vol. 1 (Jan./Feb. 1994), 25–9.

11 See the article "Personalism" in *The Westminster Dictionary of Christian Ethics* (Philadelphia: Westminster Press 1986).

12 Abraham Rotstein wrestles with this topic in "The Reality of Society: Karl Polanyi's Philosophical Perspective."

13 John Paul II, *Sollicitudo rei socialis* (1987), numbered paragraphs 15, 25, 44. For the English text and commentary, see Gregory Baum and Robert Ellsberg, eds., *The Logic of Solidarity* (Maryknoll, N.Y.: Orbis Books 1989), 13, 25, 49, 80–1.

CHAPTER 3

1 The most recent attack on the use of social science in theological ethics is John Milbank's brilliant *Theology and Social Theory* (Oxford, England: Blackwell 1991). For a critical response to John Milbank, see my *Essays in Critical Theology* (Kansas City, Mo.: Sheed and Ward 1994).

2 See Martin Jay, *The Dialectical Imagination* (Boston: Little, Brown 1973), 253–80.

3 See André Gunder Frank, *Latin America: Underdevelopment or Revolution* (New York: Modern Reader 1969).

4 Jacques Godbout, "The Self-Regulating State," in Mendell and Salée, eds., *The Legacy of Karl Polanyi*, 119–32.

5 This quotation comes from a letter written by Polanyi in 1943, cited in an unpublished paper, "Polanyi: A Theory of Needs," given by Marguerite Mendell at the Conference "La radicalité du quotidien," Université du Québec à Montréal, 1987.

6 Ibid.

7 In his recent book *L'esprit du don* (Montréal: Boréal 1992) Jacques Godbout explores Polanyi's intuition of the ongoing power of reciprocity in modern society.

8 U.S. Catholic Bishops, "Economic Justice for All" (1986), in David O'Brien and Thomas Shannon, eds., *Catholic Social Thought: The Documentary Heritage* (Maryknoll, N.Y.: Orbis Books 1992), 572–680.

9 See E.F. Sheridan, ed., *Do Justice! The Social Teaching of the Canadian Catholic Bishops* (Toronto: Jesuit Centre for Social Faith and Justice 1987), especially the statement "Ethical Reflections on the Economic Crisis" (1982), 399–410. For an analysis of the Canadian bishops' social teaching, see Gregory Baum, *Theology and Society*, "Toward a Canadian Catholic Social Theory" (New York: Paulist Press 1987), pp 66–87.

10 Alain Touraine, *The Post-Industrial Society* (New York: Random House 1971).

11 Claus Offe, *Contradictions of the Welfare State* (London: Hutchinson Education 1984).

12 Manfred Bienefeld, "Karl Polanyi and the Contradictions of the 1980s," in Mendell and Selée, eds., *The Legacy of Karl Polanyi*, 3–28.

13 Marguerite Mendell and Daniel Salée, "Introduction," *The Legacy of Karl Polanyi*, viii–xxix. The contributors to the same book who recognize the counter-movement are Brent McClinton, J. Ron Stanfield, Trent Schroyer, and Björn Hettne. Also, see the articles by J. Ron Stanfield and Björn Hettne in Polanyi-Levitt, ed., *The Life and Work of Karl Polanyi.*

14 See Louis Favreau, *Mouvements populaires et interventions communautaires de 1960 à nos jours: continuités et rupture* (Montreal: Les éditions du fleuve 1989); and, by the same author, "The 'Backyard Revolution' in Québec: People and Community in a Liberal Democracy," in Colin Leys and Marguerite Mendell, eds., *Culture and Social Change* (Montreal: Black Rose Books 1992), 200–11.

15 Economic Council of Canada, *From the Bottom Up: The Community Economic Development Approach* (Ottawa, 1990).

16 Björn Hettne, "The Contemporary Crisis: The Rise of Reciprocity," in Polanyi-Levitt, ed., *The Life and Work of Karl Polanyi*, 208–20.

17 For the proceedings of the colloquium, see Benoit Lévesque *et al.*, eds., *L'autre économie* (Presses de l'Université du Québec

1989). See also "Le dossier: l'économie alternative," *Relations*, no. 548 (March 1989), 40–54.

18 See Gregor Murray, "Union Culture and Organizational Change in Ontario and Quebec," and Mona-Josée Gagnon, "Trade Unions in Quebec: New Stakes," in Leys and Mendell, eds., *Culture and Social Change*, 39–61 and 62–74.

19 Louis Fournier, *Solidarité Inc.* (Montreal, Éditions Québec/Amérique 1991); and Diane Gabrielle Tremblay and Vincet Van Schendel, *Économie du Québec* (Montreal: Éditions Saint-Martin 1991). In Quebec, "le forum pour l'emploi" has been established by representatives of labour, business, and government to discuss the possibility of multiplying projects of *concertation.* The expression 'Quebec Inc.' was used by Gérald Tremblay, minister of industry, trade, and commerce, to designate his proposal of industrial clusters ("des grappes industrielles") distributed over the province.

20 The Quebec Conference of Bishops, "Pour vivre la démocratie économique," in *Église canadienne*, no. 25 (14 May 1992), 199–204. For an English translation, see "A Letter from Quebec," in Denise Carmody and John Carmody, eds., *The Future of Prophetic Christianity* (Maryknoll, New York: Orbis Books 1993), 94–9.

21 See *Relations*: "Le dossier: Un Québec cassé en deux," no. 545 (Nov. 1988), 264–76; "Le dossier: Pas de pays sans régions," no. 579 (April 1992), 72–84; "Le dossier: Repenser le travail," no. 650 (May 1992), 104–16; "Le dossier: Où va l'économie?" no. 587 (Jan./Feb. 1993), 8–20; "Le dossier: L'avenir de la gauche," no. 594 (Oct. 1993), 232–44; "Le dossier: Habiter la forêt," no. 598 (March 1994), 39–52.

22 Gregory Baum, "The Catholic Left in Quebec," in Leys and Mendell, eds. *Culture and Social Change*, 140–54, esp. 147–50.

CHAPTER 4

1 Charles Taylor, *Sources of the Self* (Cambridge, Mass.: Harvard University Press 1989), 31.

2 See Alain Caille, "Notes sur le concept d'utilitarisme," a paper given at the 3rd International Karl Polanyi Conference, Milan, 1990.

3 Hans Küng, *Global Responsibility: In Search of a New World Ethic* (New York: Crossroads 1991); Jacques Robin, *Changer d'ère* (Paris: Le seuil 1989).

4 The international secretariat of the World Conference on Religion and Peace is located at 777 United Nations Plaza, New York, N.Y. 10017.

5 See Jacques Godbout, *L'esprit du don.*

6 For Robert Bellah's article, "Civil Religion in America," and the debate it stirred up, see Russel Richey and Donald Jones, eds., *American Civil Religion* (New York: Harper and Row 1974).

7 See Edward Schillebeeckx, *The Schillebeeckx Reader* (New York: Crossroad 1987), 54–6.

8 Mencius, one of the best known Confucian philosophers, developed the theme that "all men have the mind that cannot bear to see the suffering of others." See Wing-tsit, ed., *A Source Book in Chinese Philosophy* (Princeton, N.J.: Princeton University Press 1963), 65.

9 Paul Ricoeur, "Responsibility and Fragility: An Ethical Reflection," *Arc*, vol. 31 (Spring 1993), 7–10.

10 Charles Wilber, "Incentives and the Organization of Work," in John Coleman, ed., *One Hundred Years of Catholic Social Teaching* (Maryknoll, N.Y.: Orbis Books 1991), 212–23.

11 See chapter 2, n. 13, above.

Index